S0-BMZ-835

babies'ROOMS
from zero to three

babies'ROOMS
from zero to three

JUDITH WILSON   photography by WINFRIED HEINZE

RYLAND
PETERS
& SMALL
LONDON NEW YORK

Designer **Pamela Daniels**
Commissioning editor **Annabel Morgan**
Location research **Tracy Ogino**
Production manager **Patricia Harrington**
Art director **Anne-Marie Bulat**
Editorial director **Julia Charles**
Publishing director **Alison Starling**

First published in the United States in
2006 by Ryland Peters & Small, Inc
519 Broadway, Fifth Floor
New York, NY 10012
www.rylandpeters.com

10 9 8 7 6 5 4 3 2 1

Text copyright © Judith Wilson 2006
Design and photographs copyright
© Ryland Peters & Small 2006

ISBN-10: 1-84597-146-9
ISBN-13: 978-1-84597-146-5

All rights reserved. No part of this
publication may be reproduced, stored in
a retrieval system, or transmitted in any
form or by any means, electronic,
mechanical, photocopying, or otherwise,
without the permission of the publisher.

Printed and bound in China

Library of Congress Cataloging-in-Publication Data

Wilson, Judith, 1962-
  Babies' rooms : from zero to three / Judith Wilson ;
with photography by Winfried Heinze.-- 1st ed.
     p. cm.
  Includes index.
  ISBN-13: 978-1-84597-146-5
  ISBN-10: 1-84597-146-9
  1. Children's rooms. 2. Interior decoration. I.
Heinze, Winfried. II.
Title.

NK2117.C4W548 2006
747.7'7--dc22

2005031111

contents

INTRODUCTION

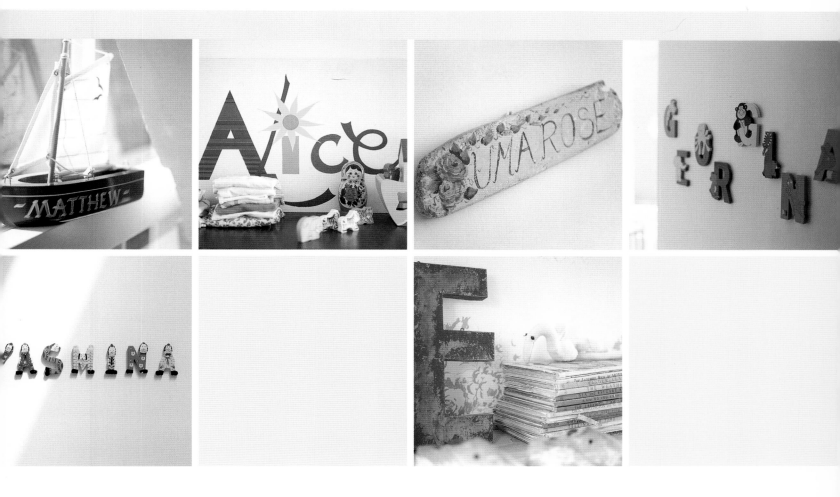

The arrival of a new baby is a major milestone. Your personal life will never be quite the same again, nor, from the moment that first teddy lands on the sofa, will the life of your home. It's vital to accept that now. But if you are able to plan for baby's new existence, using a practical eye and a sense of fun, the transition from child-free zone to dynamic family home can be seamless.

Whether you're expecting newborn number one or the arrival of a sibling, space at home—or the lack of it—is a crucial issue. It can be tempting to move house, but is that disruption really essential? It is often better to wait until you have some first-hand experience of life with a baby (or even a couple of youngsters), so you can work out exactly what constitutes your ideal living space.

Choosing equipment (and working out where it all goes) is equally pressing. Try to ignore the exhaustive list of equipment that baby stores would like you to buy. Babies have very simple needs—somewhere to sleep, a changing zone and a place to play—so focus only on essential items in the early days. For many parents, the arrival of a baby means a drop in income, so don't waste money on items that will soon be unnecessary.

Remember that, while creating a cozy bedroom for your baby is a natural, fulfilling task (and the really fun part!), minor adjustments will be needed everywhere. You'll want more storage, not to mention making space in the bathroom, the kitchen, and your bedroom for the new incumbent to share. Surfaces everywhere need to be practical, and—as baby becomes mobile—potential danger zones must be made safe.

Thankfully, it is possible to have a baby-friendly house that retains its stylish good looks. There has been a boom in well-designed kids' furniture and accessories, so whether you want cutting-edge chic or a nostalgic mood, there will be something to suit. Enjoy researching good-looking equipment and integrating it into your home.

Above all, remember that from day one your home needs to adapt as your little one grows and as new siblings arrive. Babies develop with alarming speed. In zero to three years, tots go from kicking on a mat to scooting around a playroom, from the security of a swinging cradle to the maturity of a bed. Anticipate their needs, stay true to your style, and turn a blind eye to a little bit of chaos. Welcome to family living!

SLEEPING NOOKS

Many parents prefer to keep a newborn in their own bedroom in the early days. For couples without a spare bedroom for a nursery, or those living in an open-plan apartment, such an arrangement may be a necessity. Plan your space carefully, to ensure that baby has a quiet nook of its very own and so you don't feel too invaded by the new arrival.

this page **If baby is sleeping in your room, the lighting may need some subtle changes. Add a dimmer switch to overhead lights, so you don't have to get undressed in the dark, and fit lower-wattage bulbs to bedside lamps, so you can read in bed without disturbing baby.**

Streamline the contents of your bedside table. There should be space for a stack of burp cloths, diapers, and a glass of water for you if you're breast-feeding. *opposite, top right* **Allocate a special place for soft toys, so they don't take over the entire bedroom.**

Flowers or a scented candle will provide a gentle ambience for you and baby.

Few of us are truly prepared for the reality of a new baby. We may buy all the equipment, and read the books, but the reality of a newborn—the crying, the feeding, the changing— is often a shock, not to mention the accompanying sleep deprivation. If you add to that mix limited time for organizing, perhaps the demands of siblings, and heightened emotions all around, it's not surprising things can get a little fraught.

If you have chosen to keep your baby in your bedroom, even just for a few weeks, do plan carefully to ensure that your once-peaceful zone doesn't suffer too much disruption. The advantages of having the baby close to you are manifold: you won't need to go to another room to feed or change, you can keep a watchful eye on your little one, and a baby derives great comfort from sharing a room with its parents.

When planning, consider the best position for the bassinet or cradle. In the early days, you'll want it beside the bed. Is there also room for extras, such as a breast-feeding pillow? Even if you have furnished a separate nursery for baby, it is worth keeping essentials in your room to avoid having to trek across the landing at night. A changing mat, for example, can be discreetly tucked under the bed, with toiletries for diaper changes stacked on a wheeled cart. Spare bodysuits can be piled into a wicker basket, or you could clear a space in your own chest of drawers.

below **Grown-up window treatments, such as unlined curtains, will need to be adapted so that the room can be kept dark for daytime naps. Add a plain white blackout roll-up shade, or replace sheer curtains with thick lined drapes.**

Your primary consideration will be baby's first bed. Although you'll also need a crib for the early years, a bassinet or cradle will fit in most parents' bedrooms and feels secure for a newborn. The advantage of a bassinet teamed with a stand is that it is portable, looks unfussy (provided you avoid frilly fabric linings), and is inexpensive. A rocking cradle is an excellent choice for a fussy baby, as you can soothe baby with the gentle swinging motion. A simple fabric baby hammock is another alternative.

If baby is likely to be in your room long-term, perhaps for the first year, then you could invest in a bedside crib. Designed with a pull-down side and a choice of mattress base levels, it can be placed adjacent to the parents' bed in the early days, for easy night-time feeds. Later, it can be transformed into a conventional crib. If you need to accommodate a full-size crib in the bedroom, choose one on castors that can be moved a little further from your bedside after a month or two. This gives you some physical breathing space and means baby is less likely to be disturbed when you go to bed.

below left **If baby must sleep with you long-term, consider creating a purpose-built niche along one wall. Here, built-in cupboards hold all the baby equipment, while the crib sits in the cozy alcove below. The modern crib and feeding chair have been chosen to blend with the contemporary bedroom.**

this page **An older baby sharing his or her parents' bedroom will be easily distracted by your presence in the mornings, so you will all get more sleep if there is a physical barrier between your bed and the crib. In a traditional-style room, consider tucking the crib behind a decorative three-panel screen. In a modern interior, a glass panel screened with a Venetian shade is a discreet solution. A larger room may benefit from sliding doors.**

Display your personal selection of baby pictures in conventional frames, or order a canvas printed with a favorite digital image.

this page **Provided you keep things neatly folded, everything from bodysuits to diaper-changing toiletries look good in wicker baskets with a fabric lining. An open-topped basket allows easy access.**

opposite, left **If baby is in your bedroom long-term, convert one section of your closet into a changing area. Add a mat on top of a chest of drawers, with space for a diaper disposal system.**
left **Invest in smart-looking metal, cardboard, or wicker storage boxes, which can be stacked on existing shelves to keep baby's things tidy.**

Do give due consideration to the decorative impact of the baby's bed. It certainly eases the shock of having a new incumbent if the crib harmonizes with the scheme in your bedroom. If you have blond wood detailing, choose a crib with bleached tones or in white, or if the look is modern pick a funky oval design. You can choose baby bedding and a crib bumper to match the existing color scheme. Save pattern or strong contrasts for when baby moves into his or her own room.

If space permits, it's a good idea to add an armchair or even a small sofa to the master bedroom. This provides a comfortable, tranquil spot for feeding baby during the day, or a good place for you to cuddle up with a small sibling. Brothers or sisters may feel jealous if a new baby takes root in their parents' bedroom. If children make a habit of night-time visits, it will make everyone's lives easier if you provide a soft mattress and a blanket on the other side of your bed, so they have a special place to settle in your room, too.

Do remember that, as well as creating a peaceful sleeping zone for your new baby, your bedroom must continue to provide you and your partner with respite. Treat yourself to a favorite scented candle, a new set of bed linen, and a comforting wool throw to wrap around yourself if you're up feeding baby in the night.

THE UNISEX NURSERY

Keep your plans simple for a first nursery, especially if decorating prior to the baby's birth. Concentrate on choosing the right basics, which can be added to as time goes by. If you don't know your baby's sex, there's no point fretting over pinks and blues. Think outside the box: unisex color schemes, from all white to apple, tangerine, or cherry, make a refreshing change.

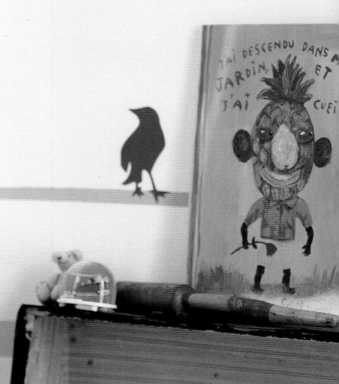

Stylized bird and flower motifs make a change from teddies.

When planning a first nursery, it's very tempting to start by plunging in and selecting a color scheme or choosing the furniture. Yet what matters more is allocating the right room for your baby. Often there's no choice: a first child goes into the only spare bedroom available. But if there are options, the ideal location is next door to your bedroom, or at the very least on the same floor, so you can hear crying and don't have to walk far in the night. Try to avoid placing the nursery *opposite, left* **A washable blanket and soft pillow make a warm and cosy alternative to a wipe-clean vinyl changing mat. While you are changing diapers, keep baby amused with an overhead mobile, a brightly stenciled motif, or soft toys at hand.**

this picture **If you want to display toys from your own childhood, or books not yet suitable for baby, group them attractively out of reach.** *right* **Jazz up plain white paintwork by cutting out bird, butterfly, or flower shapes and sticking them to the walls.**

too close to the stairs or other living quarters, so that footsteps or the television won't disturb a sleeping baby.

If you already have one child, there are some choices to be made. If he or she occupies the former spare room, consider a loft conversion, which can be more cost-effective than moving house. If an older sibling is already in the "baby" room next to yours, and there's a larger bedroom elsewhere, it may be the right time to promote a toddler to greater independence.

But if jealousy is likely, don't move the older child. Instead, convert an upstairs study or dressing room into a tiny nursery. A small attic makes a cozy first room.

Whether you are just redecorating the baby's room or doing up a whole house, consider practicalities like the lighting and other services now. You will need to control the level of electric light, so fit a dimmer switch to overhead lights. The addition of wall lights close to the crib will do away with the need for a bedside light. Do you have enough electrical sockets? As well as a baby monitor, a CD player for music, and a fan in summer, you may wish to plug in a nightlight. Anticipate safety needs now, and buy covers for all unused

Cater for the possibility of a baby girl or boy by choosing a predominantly white scheme, accented with pastel pinks and blues, and a classic mix of stripes and florals.

this page **An attic bedroom, with its sloping ceilings, makes a cosy choice for a new baby. Furnish it simply, with an armchair, a crib, and a chest of drawers. Ensure that an attic room has a decent-sized window, as well as a fan, so baby doesn't get overheated in summer.** *opposite* **Tongue and groove paneling is a crisp-looking, easy-care alternative to painted walls or wallpaper.**

Handmade accessories add instant personality to a new baby's bedroom.

this page **Choose furniture that sits well with the architecture of your home. In this nursery, the pale weatherboarded furniture blends sympathetically with the ceiling beams, while providing much-needed relief from the dark wood. Look for matching sets that will grow up with baby: for example, once the mat is removed,** **this changing unit will become a toy cupboard.** *opposite above* **In a small room, plan the layout with care. By projecting this crib diagonally, the parents have access to both sides and the room feels less poky.** *opposite below left and right* **In a dark bedroom, jolly, brightly colored accessories will lift the mood and are suitable for both sexes.**

electrical sockets. Check that both heating and ventilation are adequate: a steady temperature of 18˚C is ideal.

Most new parents will be equipping a nursery from scratch, and just purchasing the basics—the crib, storage, a chair—can be something of an investment. It's tempting to buy an entire set of matching furniture, but it really isn't essential. All too soon, a toddler will outgrow scaled-down pieces, and you'll have to start all over again. If you are set on the coordinated look, seek out ranges that are specifically designed to grow up with the child, such as those with a full-height armoire, or a matching first bed. Buy all the pieces at the same time, as some nursery ranges are discontinued with alarming speed.

You'll achieve a more personal-looking nursery, however, if you mix grown-up pieces of furniture, such as a chest of drawers and a trunk, with an attractive crib. Make the crib your first major buy. Happily, the days of the ubiquitous pine crib have gone. There are many beautifully designed styles on the market, across all price ranges, from wrought-iron styles to classic woods like oak, maple and

beech. If you don't yet know the sex of your baby, pick a classic style in plain wood or white.

Spend some time in a nursery showroom investigating the practicalities. Ideally, a crib should have three base positions and a one- or two-hand drop-side mechanism. Castors are also useful. It's personal choice whether you go for a crib or a convertible crib. If you've just started a family, then it's cost-effective to buy one good crib, which can be used by each successive baby as older siblings move on to a single bed. On the other hand, a convertible crib gives a growing toddler security, as it transforms from crib to toddler bed to full-size bed. A crib will last a baby up to two years old, whereas a convertible crib will last much longer.

You will also need an efficient diaper changing area, but don't feel under pressure to buy a changing table. It will be soon be unnecessary (though some styles are designed to convert into a toy storage unit). Either put a changing mat on top of a chest of drawers (using the top drawers for essentials like diapers, creams, and wipes), or look out for a small table with a shelf underneath. If you're decorating a baby's room from scratch, you could have a custom-made changing zone built. Some cribs come with a crib-top changer, which slots over the top of the crib and saves space in a small nursery.

In the early days there's no need for lots of storage. Of course, if you're doing a nursery from scratch, a built-in closet or free-standing armoire is ideal, long-term. Otherwise, you can get away with a capacious chest of drawers, which can hold everything from spare bedding to clothes, or an open shelf unit stacked with wicker baskets. Combine closed storage with coat hooks—great for little hats and hooded towels. Baskets or rubber tubs are perfect for soft toys and books. And a wicker or plastic laundry bin will see your child through to adulthood.

An armchair is a must, for feeding and reading bedtime stories. Any comfortable chair will do; you don't have to buy a special feeding chair. Look for a low-slung style, with good lumbar support, and low arms that won't get in the way if you're breast-feeding. Choose sensible upholstery.

Have a loose cover made in washable cotton or denim or, in a modern room, a leather chair, which will wipe clean. If there are toddler siblings, add a beanbag or soft seating cubes, so they can join in.

For a first nursery, keep things simple in decorative terms. There is plenty of time, in later years, to personalize a small child's bedroom. So stick to plain furnishings, and avoid fussy details. Painted walls, a neutral carpet, or painted floorboards, and full-length curtains in plain cotton, or shades, are ideal.

Order shades with a blackout lining, or buy ready-made blackout curtain linings to fit existing drapes.

In the first year at least, it is you—rather than your baby—who will take pleasure from the decorative scheme. An all-white combination is tranquil, and looks good with pastel or bright accessories. If you want to use color, then one wall painted in a clear bright shade, such as apple green or coral, looks fresh and pretty. Gentle pattern, in the form of gingham curtains, or an animal-print floor pillow, adds character without dominating.

opposite, left **In a small room, built-in storage will free up floor space and looks smart and modern. This clever changing station has shelves above for burp cloths and creams, and cupboards below for stacking bulkier items like spare diapers. In later years, the shelves can hold books and toys.**
opposite, right **Having a baby doesn't have to mean sacrificing style: a classic Eames chair will be comforting for rocking baby to sleep.**
this page **Choose open shelves for storing baby items that are in daily use, so you can access diapers or toiletries with one hand.**

A monochromatic scheme provides a soothing blank canvas for a new baby and its first possessions.

this page **Choose practical and soft nursery flooring, as tots will spend lots of time crawling and playing on the floor. A wool carpet is better than fibers such as sisal or coir, which can be too rough for delicate skin and don't clean well. If you've gone for a monochromatic scheme, with color splashes from toys and accessories, it's safer to pick a plain carpet, such as dove gray or biscuit. A close pile provides a satisfyingly flat surface that's ideal for balancing toys on the floor.**

left and far left **Pick a combination of storage options to suit the needs of you and your baby. In this tiny bedroom, shallow wall-mounted cupboards keep equipment and supplies well out of the baby's reach. But the bright plastic toy bin is easy for a toddler to access, and a low trunk provides space for soft toys, as well as being a convenient play surface.**

Plain, painted white walls allow you the freedom to decorate using your growing baby's artwork, with all its colorful, naive appeal.

The best way to add personality is by choosing decorative crib bedding. There is a huge choice of fun, colorful accessories. Steer clear of a fully coordinated set (and be aware that babies under 12 months must not use a pillow or a down comforter), and mix and match. Good choices include an appliquéd cotton quilt, a brightly colored fleece blanket, and perhaps a gingham or striped cotton crib bumper.

Don't overload a new baby's room with too many accessories. A baby is just as happy watching dancing sunbeams as a carefully executed painting, and it takes time to fill up a new little person's room with their own special things. Add a shelf to show off cute toys and christening gifts. These days there's an increasing vogue for personalized gifts for babies. A painted wooden initial, a crib blanket embroidered with baby's birth date, or even a toy from your own childhood, will all provide an excellent starting point.

ROOMS FOR GIRLS

Pink is the ultimate color choice for girls and, with such a range of attractive hues, from shell to raspberry, it gives you the flexibility to go traditional or modern. Clear, bright shades, from acid yellow to turquoise, can look equally pretty. Design your baby girl's room to evolve with her, so concentrate on combining grown-up feminine touches with a sense of fun.

A plain white mat and a wicker basket to hold diapers creates a discreet changing zone.

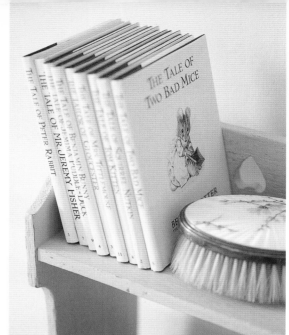

opposite, right **A grown-up chest of drawers, repainted in white, cream, or a gentle pastel shade, can double up as a changing table. Deep drawers hold clothing, spare bedding, and baby toiletries.**

below right **This attic bedroom is girly without being contrived. The simple white furniture and the Plantation-style shutters counteract the sweetness of the pale pink painted walls.**

right **A small shelf, positioned out of your baby's grasp, is a good place to display christening treasures and classic books.**

Whether you're decorating for a little girl on the way, or planning a nursery for a baby girl graduating from her bassinet, knowing the sex of your baby makes a difference. However politically correct we may wish to be, few of us can resist the temptation of color-coding. Our grown-up fashion and design tastes may be cool and trendy, but it's hard to resist the charm of little girls' pink accessories.

The secret, of course, is to steer a tasteful course through the lurid pink and fairy-emblazoned merchandise in the stores, and devise a subtle yet charming decorative scheme. Whether you go traditional, chic, or modern is up to your personal style. But remember that your little girl's room should harmonize with the rest of the décor at home. If the look elsewhere is elegant, with linen drapes and dark wood floors, take this as your starting point and lighten the scheme using pale pastel colors *below* **Simple window treatments can be dressed up with a decorative curtain pole, such as this barley-twist design, or choose a modern metal pole with a colorful glass ball or flower-motif finial.**

right **For a baby girl's nursery, a flower-print wallpaper looks** irresistibly pretty. Pick a decent-size motif, as tiny sprigs can look indistinct on the walls. For a retro look, opt for a gently faded design.

opposite, left **Much-loved family treasures, such as a rocking horse or a cross-stitch sampler, add instant personality to a little girl's bedroom.**

and satin ribbon detailing. In a trendy household, with retro 20th-century furniture, incorporate a piece in the nursery, and use vintage fabrics for curtains.

On the birth of a first child, it may seem that the baby stage will go on forever. But very quickly that baby turns into a toddler and then a little girl with definite opinions. So plan with an eye on the future, and add flexibility to your scheme. You may love Cinderella-style bedroom furniture, but a tomboy two-year-old may not approve. Equally, a modern built-in nursery in muted colors can look quite bizarre filled with fluffy pink accessories. So try not to be too extreme in your design choices.

Choose key pieces in a classic design; then, as years go by, you can change the look of the room using new paint colors, wallpaper, and bedding.

The crib is the inevitable focus in a little girl's bedroom. If you're buying for a first-born daughter, and think the crib may be needed for a boy later, look for pretty, yet not overtly girly detailing. Scroll carving, scalloped contours, or elegantly curved ends on the head- and foot-boards are all appropriate. If you're buying a convertible crib for your daughter, you can adopt a more feminine look. A wooden or sleigh-bed style with simple heart or star cut-out detailing will please a growing toddler without looking too

top and above **Little girls don't really need a huge wardrobe (save that for later years!) and their clothes are so adorable they deserve to be on display. Hang little dresses from door hooks, hat-stands, and painted wooden coat hooks.**

For a contemporary spin on the classic girl's color scheme, combine bright lipstick-pink with bold shades like scarlet, graphite, and apple green.

right **When planning a scheme, do take into account any dominant architectural features. This loft apartment, with its high ceilings and large windows, required strong blocks of color and bold modern motifs to balance the over-sized proportions. Comforting textures, from the dense carpet pile to the floppy, fleecy floor pillows, make it cozy for a toddler. While it's fun for a little one to have lots of floor space to play on, in a big room ensure that the crib is placed against one wall so that the child feels a sense of enclosure and safety.**

cutesy. If you're stuck with a very plain crib, then a mosquito net or gingham canopy adds a pretty touch.

Once your baby girl gets beyond the crib stage, you have choices. For little ones that crave security, what are often termed "toddler beds" are ideal. Toddler beds help a child make the transition from a crib to a regular bed. They are close to the ground and have an integral bed guard. For a traditional look, choose a wooden style, with classic detailing or, for a more contemporary finish, a slatted head- and foot-board.

If you have a child who is happy to go straight into a bed, invest in a single bed to last her up to her teens. Look for a classic style that will grow with her, like an upholstered divan (which can be updated with new fabric in later years), an antique-style wrought-iron bed, or a modern bed with under-bed storage. Long before baby graduates from her crib, you can place the bed in the room. It will provide somewhere for you to sleep during a disturbed night, and your little one can slowly get used to the idea of a grown-up bed.

above **Adding a tiny play table and chairs to a nursery makes life more interesting for babies just learning to walk, and is a cozy place for toddlers to draw or give a doll's tea party.**

left **Abstract prints, in bold primary colors, make a bright splash on plain white walls.**

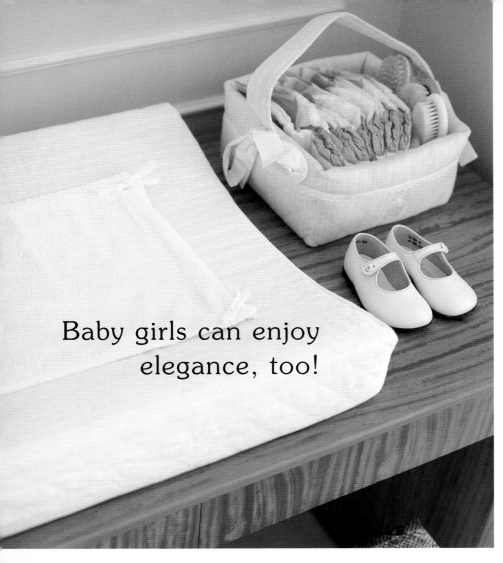

Baby girls can enjoy elegance, too!

Enjoy dressing up your baby's crib or bed with attractive linens, but don't overload it: most children don't like much bedding. For a baby, the basics are a fitted sheet and cotton blankets. A first bed might need a pillow, a comforter, scatter pillows, and a quilt or blanket on top. The colors and patterns you choose will affect the overall look of the room, particularly if the rest of the decoration is simple. If you've gone for a cool white scheme, add a girly touch using strong pastel plains in shades like grass or lilac. For a classic finish, a decorative crib quilt, featuring patchwork, appliqué, or

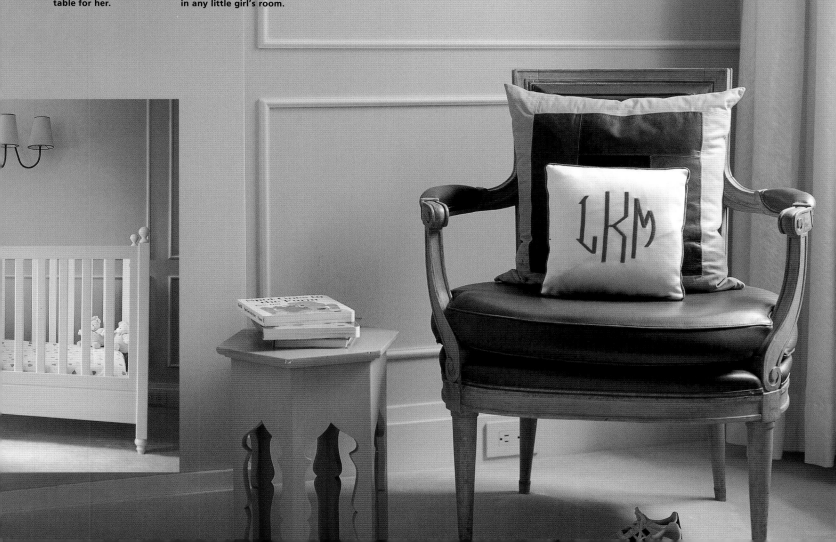

opposite, above and below A low, wide console table, teamed with a stool, makes a sensible choice for a changing table. This beautiful combination, teaming chic wood with snakeskin upholstery, is the perfect example of long-term planning, as when baby grows up the table will become a dressing table for her.

below, centre **Positioned** suitably low over the crib, and fitted with a dimmer switch, a wall light gives a comforting glow at night and can't be knocked over by a busy toddler.

this page **A pillow** bearing baby's birth date and full name, or a monogrammed cushion deserves pride of place in any little girl's room.

embroidery, provides warmth and may come with a matching crib bumper. Detailing like ric-rac braid, scalloped edges, and monograms look both pretty and chic.

While it's fun to add pattern using bedding (and these days the sky's the limit on motifs, from cupcakes and fairies to hearts and flowers), do try to avoid using a fully coordinated range with matching quilt, curtains, and lampshade. Your aim is to personalize the room, not make it look like a room set. Using pattern on the walls sets a particularly dominant theme. Traditional floral wallpaper looks prettily nostalgic, while bold, stylized flowers would suit a

Bright, energizing shades are as appealing for little girls as traditional pink, and make a great background for primary-colored toys.

above, left and center **A bedroom should be a peaceful zone to sleep in, but there must still be things to look at. While a baby will enjoy a mobile, toddlers relish ceiling-hung attractions such as wooden birds, paper dragons, and papier mâché "makes." Add plenty of shelves for bedtime books.**

left and this page **Getting the scale right in the bedroom goes a long way towards creating a cozy atmosphere for little people. This bedroom, tucked beneath a mezzanine floor in a double-height city apartment, has been tailor-made to suit its small owner. The little bed is close to the ground, as are the open shelves, making it easy to access toys. The touch-catch mechanism on the doors of the large storage unit keeps grown-up things out of her grasp.**

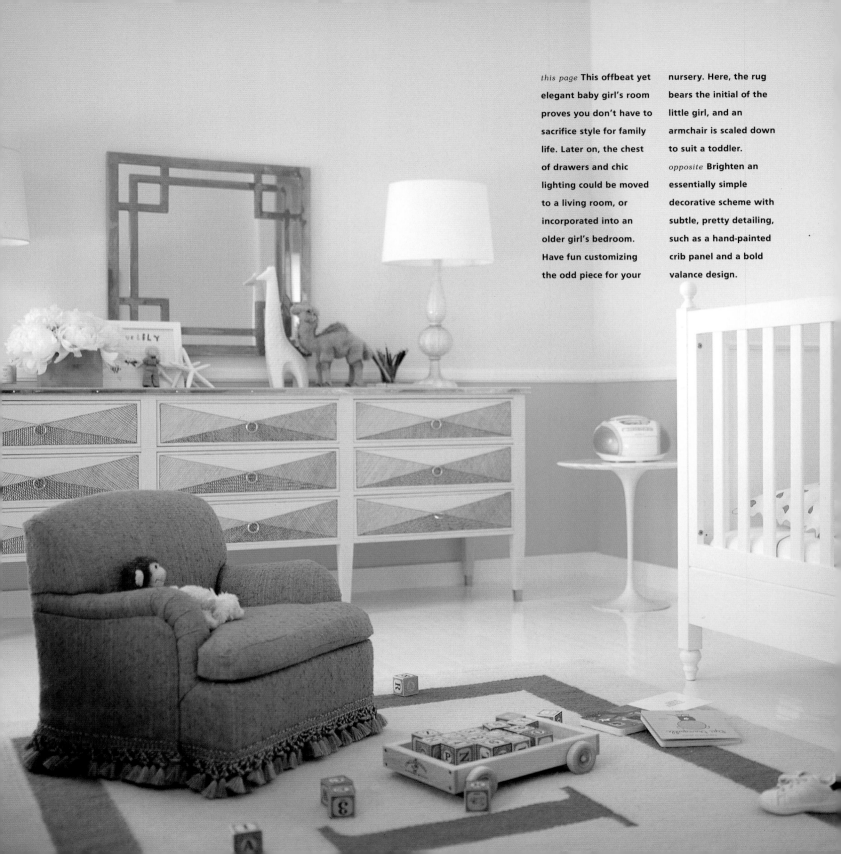

this page **This offbeat yet elegant baby girl's room proves you don't have to sacrifice style for family life. Later on, the chest of drawers and chic lighting could be moved to a living room, or incorporated into an older girl's bedroom. Have fun customizing the odd piece for your** nursery. **Here, the rug bears the initial of the little girl, and an armchair is scaled down to suit a toddler.**
opposite **Brighten an essentially simple decorative scheme with subtle, pretty detailing, such as a hand-painted crib panel and a bold valance design.**

contemporary interior. A hand-painted border, in a pastel color, sits well with white-washed furniture and a modern-country mood.

If you don't want to use pattern, it's still possible to set an unusual decorative tone with color. Pink isn't mandatory, but it does have its advantages—it's easy on the eye, most little (and big) girls love it, and you can interpret it across a vast range. Steer clear of traditional pale pinks, and look at a paint chart to remind yourself of the many variations. For the trendiest take,

choose one pastel-pink painted wall, teamed with lilac, which looks great with dark wood furniture. For a moodier slant (and an excellent accompaniment to hand-painted pieces), choose pale gray for walls, with raspberry upholstery. But don't be a slave to pink if it doesn't appeal. You can still achieve a pretty girl's room using brights like leaf green, egg-yolk yellow, or scarlet.

Unless you're after a very pared-down modern look (in which case, roll-up shades or shutters are ideal), a girl's room offers the opportunity *below* **If you don't want to opt for traditional floral or gingham fabrics, then abstract motifs like circles or hearts make a very cute alternative.**

right **For a bedroom that will evolve tastefully as your daughter grows from a baby into a little girl, choose simple white walls, a wooden floor, and white or wooden furniture. It is a child's ever-increasing selection of possessions, from framed prints to quirky chairs, that will add a sense of personality and vibrancy of color.**

Framed baby close-ups add personality to a nursery.

above **Tucked into the corner, with a softly upholstered headboard, this cozy bed will be welcoming for a two-year-old, but will also be suitable for an older child, too. An upholstery fabric in a bright pastel shade coordinates easily with most patterned bed linens.**

to indulge in decorative window treatments. Full-length curtains teamed with a blackout shade or fitted with a blackout lining always look pretty. Choose a simple, unfussy style—pinch pleats or tie-top headings are ideal. Stick to plains, gingham, or a simple floral, rather than nursery motif material. Good curtains are expensive, and your child will outgrow baby fabrics all too quickly. Instead, dress up a pair of plain curtains with subtle detailing such as pin-tucks, a decorative pelmet, or a contrast color or ribbon border.

Every self-respecting baby girl has an ever-growing array of clothes and shoes, all of which must be stored. As well as everyday wear, there will be special-occasion dresses and hand-knitted sweaters, not to mention clothes about to be grown into (or just grown out of). A chest of drawers is perfect. If you want one with feminine detail, either paint a junk-store find in a washed-out pastel, or look for a modern one featuring a pretty scallop edge or heart cut-out detail. Glass-fronted drawers show off stacked clothes very nicely.

A built-in closet or free-standing armoire is ideal for dresses and coats. Wicker baskets or fabric-lined boxes can be tucked into the bottom of a closet to organize shoes. If there's no room for an armoire, a wall-mounted shelf with a coat hooks beneath will allow you to display tiny shoes and her prettiest dresses. And don't forget a wall-mounted mirror, hung low down, which she will find endlessly diverting.

Don't overdo the accessories in your daughter's room, so that, as she's given treasures of her own, the room will evolve naturally. Start the collection with a few personal pieces: frame up a black-and-white baby photograph, her hand-print, and so on. And, while it's wonderful to include frivolous, girly detailing, exercise some restraint. Every little girl, from a very early age, should learn that less is always more.

above left and right **When choosing a first bed, look for styles with curved side panels that will stop a child falling out of bed. Ease a little girl into a new bed by providing cozy textures to cuddle up with. Comforters, cotton quilts, and soft blankets are a good choice.**

Dressing-up clothes can look very pretty left out on display.

above **As well as a full-height wardrobe for hanging clothes, try to incorporate as much low-level storage as possible. Built-in benches, with a lift-up lid, or a traditional toy chest, provide excellent storage for dressing-up clothes, soft toys, and bulkier dolls' equipment, and are easily accessed.**

Have fun devising a baby boy's bedroom with a spirit of adventure or a touch of whimsy, but don't forget it must feel safe and cozy, too. Stick to solid furniture, plainly styled, and a simple layout, so that busy little boys have maximum space for running around. Think beyond classic blues and add dayglo bright shades, natural textures, or modern white to your palette.

ROOMS FOR BOYS

this page and opposite, left This modern little boy's bedroom proves that, without a single nursery motif in sight, you can still create a whimsical bedroom. Here, the fun comes from the primary-colored walls, the striped rug, and design-classic wall hooks, while the jolly fabric elephant hood adds a dash of fantasy. If you are design-conscious, keep the theme going in the baby's room. With their gentle curves, this table, stool, and convertible crib are elegant enough for grown-up tastes, and safe for little ones. *opposite, right* A mobile changing table on castors can be moved around the nursery as necessary.

In the early months, there's little difference between putting together a baby boy's room and a baby girl's. The nursery you create for either sex should be a peaceful haven, as well as a gently stimulating place for baby to play when awake. Yet the room you plan now should cater for your son at least until he's three. During that time, he'll change from a gurgling infant to a busy little boy with very different needs. Boys aren't always rowdier than girls, but if you plan for a bit of rough and tumble in the nursery, everyone can relax.

Traditionally, boys have had something of a raw deal when it comes to bedrooms. For a start,

it's tempting to assume that tiny boys won't notice their surroundings. Yet your son has just as much right to a beautiful room as a girl, and so, as his parents, do you! Also, it can be harder for moms (who, odds are, will be doing the scheme) to get excited about devising what they assume must be a blue room, with the inevitable cars and stripes. But you don't have to stick to a conventional scheme. These days there are an increasing number of whimsical decorative ranges for tots, from deep-sea creatures and jungle animals to city skylines, any of which will create an imaginative spring-board for a little boy's room.

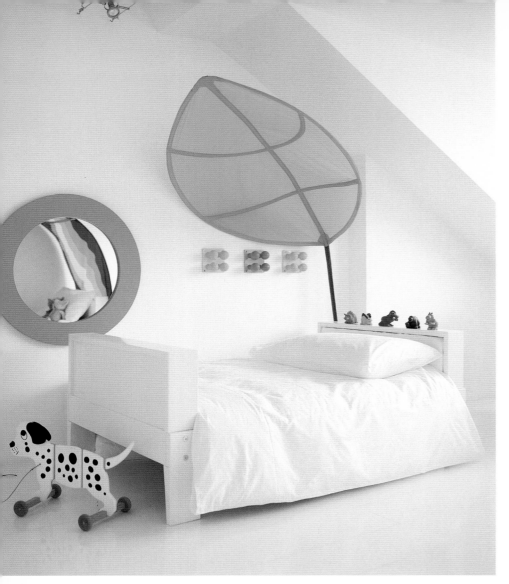

A pure white scheme, planned with simple shapes, is the ideal background for the inevitable collection of brightly colored toys.

Do remember not to go too grown-up, too soon. You (or dad) may love the idea of a sports theme, with football-emblazoned bedding, or an army bedroom, with camouflage motifs. But save these for a school-age child, who will appreciate their significance (and cool factor). In the baby years, it's more fun for your little one if he can identify simple images in his bedroom, such as sailboats and farm animals. Colors should be refreshing and clear. Boys have a lifetime of murky colors ahead, from gray sweatpants to navy suits, so let them enjoy fun shades while they can.

The key nursery furniture pieces must work hard, so buy them before you devise your color scheme. In

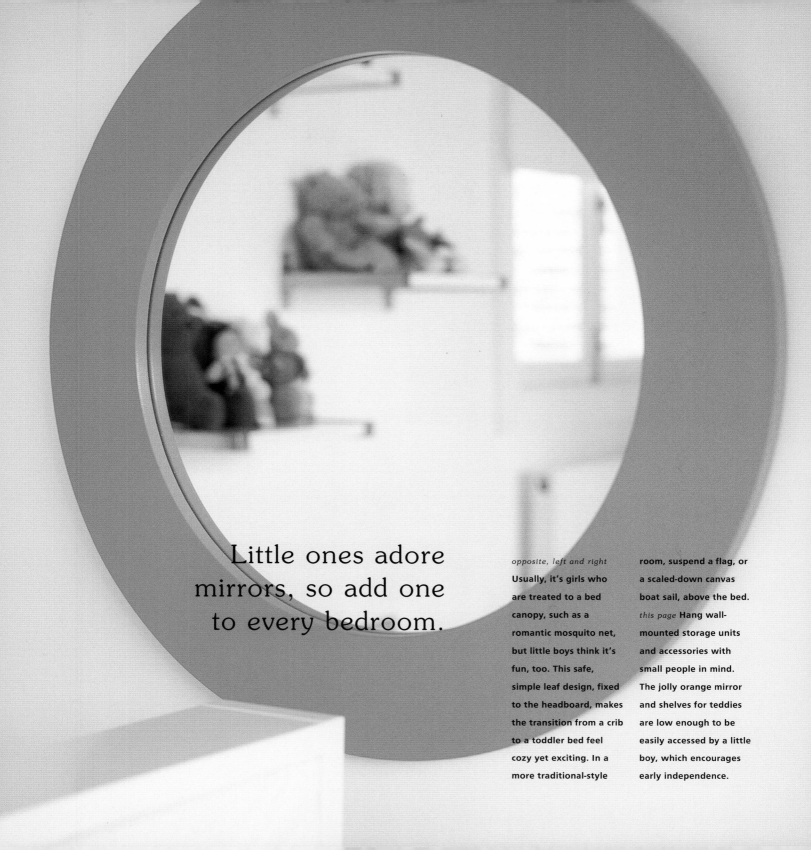

Little ones adore mirrors, so add one to every bedroom.

opposite, left and right **Usually, it's girls who are treated to a bed canopy, such as a romantic mosquito net, but little boys think it's fun, too. This safe, simple leaf design, fixed to the headboard, makes the transition from a crib to a toddler bed feel cozy yet exciting. In a more traditional-style room, suspend a flag, or a scaled-down canvas boat sail, above the bed.** *this page* **Hang wall-mounted storage units and accessories with small people in mind. The jolly orange mirror and shelves for teddies are low enough to be easily accessed by a little boy, which encourages early independence.**

this page **A brightly colored pattern, be it wallpaper or fabric, provides an easy decorative starting point for a boy's nursery scheme. Here, the retro-style cowboy wallpaper has inspired scarlet and bright-blue accent shades. A plain wooden crib, a three-legged stool for storytime, and a shelf for clothes and favorite little possessions provide all the necessary basics in a newborn boy's bedroom.**

opposite **It's fun to personalize a baby's room with special accessories. Many baby-gift mail-order catalogs offer a made-to-order service, and can add names and a memorable date to anything from bed covers to cushions or a painted canvas.**

many ways, the crib style you choose for a boy is particularly crucial, because—once you're past the tiny baby stage—you (and he) won't want it to look too pretty. Opt for the plainest crib you can find. Squared off foot- and head-ends look more restrained, as do paneled ends. Avoid a crib with cute engraved motifs, such as teddies, which may be deemed babyish by a small boy. As he moves to toddlerhood, a plain crib can be perked up with a clip-on fabric canopy in the shape of an animal head or a giant leaf.

It's a good idea to pick a wooden crib, rather than one with a white-painted finish. The inevitable knocks won't show up quite so much, and wood's natural tones will work well with bright colors or more subdued tones, from blue to olive green. These days, there's a good choice of wood veneers, including birch, oak, and beech, as well as inexpensive pine. If you have the budget, and want something really special, some children's furniture companies will create a custom-made crib in a wood of your choice. If you prefer a painted crib, then a color-washed tongue and groove style, or one with a distressed finish, is a good choice.

Boys love the security of their crib just as much as girls, but they may want to graduate to the excitement of a full-size bed more quickly. This can pose a problem, given that a small boy may fancy the delights of a bunk bed long before he is old enough to use one safely! Rather

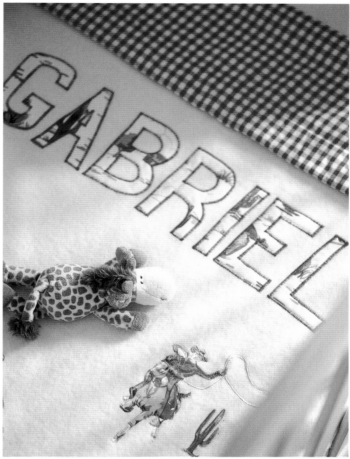

Pictorial wallpaper, featuring plenty of action, will have enduring appeal for a little boy.

than suffer the expense of a crib, then a toddler bed, it can make better sense to invest in a convertible crib then, when your little boy reaches five, he can move straight to the lower level of a bunk bed that will last him to the teenage years. If he moves from a crib to a single bed, then a built-in bed at a low level, or a sleigh bed, is a safe choice.

Remaining furniture should be chosen with practicality and fun in mind, but it must also be safe. Once little boys can walk, they can also climb. Anticipate potential hazards by choosing sturdy pieces that can't be tipped over. For example, a solid chest of drawers with a changing mat on top is better than a changing table with open shelves, as they will *left* **In a tiny attic nursery, a wall devoted to built-in shelves and cupboards creates a tranquil, modern look. If you're planning and building while your baby is still in a crib, decide in advance where a first bed will go.**

become a tempting mountain to scale. Furniture on castors can be wheeled around for fun, but is practical (for you) for maneuvring with one hand at the baby stage, too. Tall, thin items, such as a bookshelf, should be securely fixed to the wall. Choose a low chair, so little boys aren't tempted to climb up and over the other side. A giant beanbag is an alternative, as are big floor pillows.

It may seem sexist, but little boys really don't need a proper wardrobe. Tiny jeans and T-shirts are best in a chest of drawers or stacked in a painted steel locker-style cabinet. When choosing storage for a toddler, make sure drawers glide open easily, and that they are not too deep, otherwise clothes get muddled. Long, thin D-handles, chunky knobs, or cut-out apertures are all easy for chubby hands to grasp later on. Go low, so tots can access all the drawers. Wall hooks are great for a bathrobe or fleece. If your son has a really tiny bedroom, look out for cribs and beds with drawers underneath. Or invest in canvas storage containers to hold toys and shoes.

Add a built-in niche for necessities like a cup or books.

left and opposite, below
For a streamlined environment, clutter must be kept at bay. Here, toys are easy to access, yet simple to put away in under-bed storage, and a wall-mounted light and niche means there's no need for a bedside table.

Antique children's beds often come in comfortingly tiny proportions, so can make an ideal choice for a first bed once a child graduates from his crib.

Aim for a nursery layout that frees up as much floor space as possible. This means there's more room for a baby to crawl around or play, and less chance of you (or him) tripping over pieces of furniture. It's always cosier for a crib or first bed to be aligned against one wall, or tucked into a corner. You might even consider devoting an entire wall to a built-in wardrobe, storage unit, and flip-down changing zone. Always provide a bookshelf, because every baby amasses a multitude of books from day one. Fix it very low down, so your little one can help himself to favorite volumes, or gather books into a shallow basket to tuck under the crib.

Decoratively speaking, it's important to concentrate on creating a characterful scheme that your baby will grow up to enjoy, rather than a cleverly put together themed bedroom. Save that for older children, who will get more fun out of it. In these early years, concentrate on eye-catching shades and cheerful motifs. Colors that make you feel uplifted will please your baby, too. White, teamed with splashes of citrus such as lime or tangerine, is fun and modern; consider white walls with a brightly colored wool carpet. For a more traditional mood, by all means choose blue, but choose a variation on the palette. Pale-blue chalky walls look fantastic with accents of scarlet and natural wood, or a true denim blue, used for upholstery, looks fresh with white-painted paneling.

If you are longing to use patterned wallpaper—and there are now many charming designs on the market, from lighthouses to starships—then it looks more modern to use it just on one wall. Pick out one of the chief colors, then use it as a contrasting paint shade on the remaining walls. More unusually, you could wallpaper the ceiling: babies spend a lot of time on their backs, so deserve something interesting to look at. If you want less pattern, scrutinize fabric ranges for a memorable textile, which may be made up into a Roman blind or used to upholster a nursery armchair.

left **If you don't want pastels, deep tones like purple or navy, or splashes of a bright primary color such as red, can still be suitable for little boys' rooms. The trick is to mix strong colors with pale tones to keep things fresh. In this little boy's room, a panel of bold scarlet is combined with white walls and painted floorboards, so it doesn't look too overpowering.**

above left **A little boy doesn't necessarily need a proper bedside table, complete with electric lamp, just because he has moved into a bed. But a tiny table, with room for a cup and some favorite books, can be a useful extra.**

above right **Shelves can be used to display treasured baby toys and special gifts in the early years, then gradually filled with books as your little boy grows.**

far left **If a crib or bed is placed directly beneath a window, plan window treatments sensibly. You'll need a blackout shade or well-fitting shutters to keep out the light. Choose simple window treatments for little boys. A crisp, tailored Roman blind in denim, cotton, or a narrow stripe is an excellent choice, as are Plantation-style shutters. For safety's sake, keep any blind cords short.**
left and opposite **Give due importance to a little boy's treasured collection of soft toys, from teddies to hand-knitted presents from Grandma. Don't overload the bed: cluster a few favorites on the pillow and tuck the rest into a bedside basket or trunk.**

A mix of antique furniture, plus some painted junk-store finds, makes a relaxed and sensible choice for energetic little boys.

Funky bedding ranges, teamed with plain walls, are another rich source of fun nursery motifs. Don't overdo the pattern. In a little boy's room, narrow stripes, bold gingham, or big checks are great coordinates to mix in.

Finally, don't forget the tactile factor. Tiny boys, just like little girls, love to snuggle up in soft, warming textures, and it's up to you to provide plenty of cocooning fabrics. There's plenty of time, later on, for rough, tough canvas and denim. Treat your little boy to a fleecy blanket on the bed, a thick rug to play on—a target, alphabet, or modern stripe design always looks good—and he will grow up feeling that his bedroom is a safe, comforting place to be.

Stripes and checks, in shades of blue or red, are a classic and attractive combination for boys.

Whether twins will be sharing a room, or you're moving a baby in with a toddler sibling, careful planning will ensure a good night's sleep for them both. It's fun to share, but little people often have varying sleep patterns, not to mention the need for a private space all of their own. Plenty of storage—so it's easy to tidy, and peaceful at night—is the key.

SHARED ROOMS

right **In this attic bedroom for two little girls, there's little space for freestanding furniture. To keep the look uncluttered, high bedsteads provide an area beneath for storing out-of-season clothes, while a built-in closet at the opposite end of the room utilizes under-eaves space. If there's room on a landing just outside a shared room, this can be a good spot for a chest of drawers or a large armoire.**

below **Little children don't need a bedside light, and they're easily knocked over. In this traditional bedroom, a vintage wall sconce looks nostalgic, and provides a soft glow.**

right **Novelty coat hooks, either in a Shaker-style painted wood design or in metal with cute motifs, are always a winner with little ones. Hang them low on the wall, so they can reach their own clothes, and learn to tidy up.**

For most parents, the issue of sharing won't arise until baby number two (or three!) is on the way, and it's apparent that there are no more spare bedrooms. If there are twins due, a shared space is essential from day one. Those who find it tricky to get an overexcited child off to sleep may be horrorstruck at the prospect of a new baby joining the fray, but careful planning can work wonders. Well-arranged space, with tranquil decoration, goes a long way towards calmer bedtimes.

If a bedroom is too small, neither child has enough personal space. So evaluate whether the room you've chosen can cope, not just with two cribs or beds, but double the number of possessions. Draw up a floor plan, with to-scale drawings of furniture, and move them around to find the most streamlined arrangement. Review all available bedrooms: does it make more sense, for example, for you to devote the main bedroom to a shared bedroom/playroom, while you create a new parents' suite in the loft? Might two tiny rooms be knocked into one? If you have only two bedrooms but three children, don't necessarily allocate the single room to the oldest child or the baby. Let the lightest sleeper have the room of his or her own.

Moving a new baby into an older child's bedroom must be approached with sensitivity. Tiny children are *this page* **Pep up a neutral scheme, suitable for a boy and girl sharing, using identical but contrast-colored sets of bedding. Instead of pastel pink and blue, choose shades that are acceptable to either sex, such as powder blue or raspberry red with lime detailing. For variety within a tightly coordinated color scheme, choose bedding in a mix of stripes, checks, and gingham; patterns that are suitable for boys or girls.** *opposite* **For a boy and girl twin, a spacious shared armoire provides plenty of clothes storage. Inexpensive drawer units have been covered with color-coded wallpaper, but you could also use plain paint.**

If it is big enough, design a shared room with lots of free floor space, so it can double as a play zone.

quite territorial, and won't take kindly to having their personal space cluttered with a crib and a new baby. Also, try to avoid putting your toddler into a new bed while simultaneously settling the baby into the newly vacated, much-loved crib. Make the alterations in stages, and sweeten the pill for the older child by adding new bedding or a special bedside rug.

It's important to find the right spot for each bed. If you're arranging a room with a crib and a single bed, each sleeping zone may have different criteria. If a baby wakes frequently in the night, you'll want to position the crib near to the door, so you don't disturb a sleeping toddler. In a loft room, tuck the older child's bed beneath a sloping ceiling and

Mix together each child's treasures for a colorful and varied display.

position the crib in a full-head-height area of the room, so you can comfortably see to the baby's needs. It's great to divide up a room fairly, but a baby won't notice if he or she is tucked into a corner. Let your older child have the lion's share of floor space, and a window to peep out of, too.

Twin babies, or siblings close in age, will derive comfort from being able to see each other at night, so will prefer cribs or beds close to each other, either positioned in parallel or in an L-shape. In between the two cribs, place a changing table, or a low chest of drawers. Toddlers in beds will enjoy having an armchair between the beds, for bedtime stories. It's a good idea to have one wall light or low-voltage ceiling light above each bed—controlled by a different switch on a dimmer—so that if one child is sleeping, and the other is awake, you have decent illumination.

If little children share, but disturb one another, the solution may be physically screening off each sleeping zone.

opposite, left **A bulletin board is an excellent home for children's artworks and treasures. Opt for a metal or cork board, or use colorful felt or a large map for a cheerful background.**

opposite, right **If you only have room for one chest of drawers in a shared room, allocate the lower drawers to the toddler, and stash away baby clothes and supplies in the upper ones.**

above **Deep open shelves that run the whole length of one wall mean that little ones can use their bedroom as a playroom, since toys, storybooks, and puzzles are easy to access.**

Combine a
bedroom and
play corner for
the best use of
available space.

opposite **Although this shared little girls' bedroom has a predominantly hot pink color scheme, the bold splashes of bright egg-yolk yellow and a multi-colored rug ensure that the inevitable primary-colored toys don't look out of place.**

this page **Low twin beds, well within sight of one another, make a much more sociable shared bedroom arrangement for little girls than bunk beds. The crisp pink-and-white color scheme can easily adapt to more sophisticated accessories as the girls grow older.**

In a large room, you might divide up the space using a floor-to-ceiling storage unit, with cupboards, shelves, and even a porthole to make it fun. If a baby and toddler can't physically see one another once in bed, they will settle more easily. In a modern house, sliding partitions can be pushed aside by day, then transform the room into two tiny sleeping zones at night. A pretty and simple solution is to add a ceiling-hung mosquito net to both beds or cribs.

Whether you choose one closet, either built-in or free-standing, for the children to share, or give each child a sense of identity with their own chest of drawers, depends on the size of the room. If space is tight, it makes more sense to devote one wall to built-in closets. Unless children are very different in age, it's likely they will share toys and books, so combined storage is ideal. Every child, even a tiny one, likes to keep

a few precious things separate. Provide each one with a wall-mounted shelf near their bed or crib for their treasures.

If same-sex siblings or identical twins share, it can be fun to choose a scheme for an all-girl or all-boy room. A nursery with two sets of everything, from bed linen to cribs, looks very cozy. If you have a baby and a toddler, search out a nursery range with a matching crib and toddler bed, or buy identical convertible cribs. Add personality to each child's area. Hang a painting, or a wooden initial, or choose reversible bed linen, so that each bed displays a different pattern in a common color. Pillows, a rug, or a hand-knitted blanket, in contrasting shades for each bed, also inject variety.

By contrast, when a girl and a boy share, it's important to pick a decorative scheme that works for both. You may not wish to go down

left, right, and below

In this large bedroom, shared by a baby boy and his older sister, each has an appropriate sleeping zone on either side of the room. While the little girl has the freedom of a pretty iron bed, chest of drawers, and the window, the boy's corner has been made cool and fun with vintage toys, maps, and sailing memorabilia.

this page **This little boys' room has been traditionally decorated to blend with a period house yet retains a sense of fun, with hand-painted names on the door and strong blue walls. While all storage is shared—the antique armoire holds toys, with a chest of drawers for clothes—by placing the tiny beds at each side of the room, each boy has a sense of privacy. A mosquito net above each bed feels cozy when let down at night.**

the pink-for-girls and blue-for-boys route, but many accessories still come in those colors. So white or neutral walls are a good choice, as you can add lilacs and reds to the girl's zone, and indigo and orange to the boy's space, in the form of bedding, pillows, and so on. Alternatively, choose wallpaper, curtain fabric, or bed linen in a color or with a motif that both little ones will enjoy. If you want color on the walls, certain shades suit both sexes. Sherbet yellow, azure, warm apricot, and leaf green are all jolly choices.

Babies and children have little personalities from birth. In a shared room, celebrate their individuality by showing off treasured possessions. So provide a bulletin board close to each child's bed for postcards, photos, and artworks. Even little ones like to distinguish whether their, or their sibling's, area is a girl's, or a boy's, zone. Flags, airplanes, chunky furniture, and cheerful colors will delineate a boy's territory, while fairies, butterflies, and flowers are instant code for a girl's special patch.

above, left to right **Even tiny children will soon start to recognize the significance of their own name or their initials. Individualize two identical toddler beds by providing a personalized blanket for each child, hand-painting their name on the headboard, or adding a named toy close to the bed.**

BATHROOMS

All a baby really needs for bathing is a plastic bath and soft towels, so clear a space in the main bathroom for toiletries and bath toys. Toddlers, by contrast, require splashproof surfaces and lots of room to have fun, so plan for that. Create a welcoming and efficient family bathroom, with plenty of storage and safety features for little people, and you'll find the effort is well worth the investment.

right **This modern bathroom in a loft extension proves that with streamlined bathroom fixtures you can tuck a kids' bathroom into a tiny space. The deep bathtub makes bathtime fun for little children. When insetting a bathtub into a tiled area, add a deep shelf around the perimeter for toys and toiletries. Have fun choosing towels and (below) washcloths. You don't have to select cartoon-emblazoned styles: instead go for strong colors, abstract patterns, or softer pastel shades. Beach towels offer good choices.**

A compact attic bathroom is perfect for little ones.

For a new parent, having a tiny, slippery crying infant to undress and bathe can be horribly stressful. Later on, children's bathtime becomes one of the best bits of the day, a time to have fun and chat, as well as get clean. So check now whether your existing facilities will work effectively with little ones around.

In an ideal world, most parents would prefer to have a master bathroom for themselves, and another bathroom for children and guests. If there is only one small bathroom, could it be made bigger, perhaps by stealing space from an adjacent bedroom? A growing family will reap the benefit of more space, perhaps allowing for twin sinks or

a shower. If you have a spare bedroom, or are planning a loft conversion and can install a new one, it's well worth creating a children's bathroom.

In the early days, you need little for bathing baby. A plastic or bucket-style baby bath is essential. Some baths come with stands or fit across the top of the family bathtub, but it makes more sense to place it on the floor. This way, you can lay out all the necessary toiletries and towels and bathe baby in a comfortable kneeling position. Pick a baby bath to match your bathroom or, if you have an all-white scheme, choose a zingy color, with towels to match.

You'll also need a wash bowl and something to hold essentials like

above **Even tiny babies need a starter kit for grooming. Include a hairbrush, toothbrush, nail scissors, cotton balls, and baby massage oils. Choose a lockable cabinet to store a thermometer, medicine, and other basics.**

Plan a family bathroom with plenty of hard-working storage for all the kids' things. An all-white scheme accessorized with jellybean colors suits everyone.

below **This cleverly designed family bathroom, with a double-ended bathtub tucked to one side, has lots of space for kids to run around, or in which to bath baby on the floor. The waist-height counter is wide enough to take a changing mat, but in later years can double as a laundry-sorting surface. Every family bathroom needs a laundry basket and a flip-top wastebasket.**

diaper creams, baby powder, and nail scissors. Many plastic bathtubs come with a set of baby care items to match, but it's more fun to choose your own. Stock up on washcloths, hooded towels, and bath mats, and keep all these essentials close at hand. Clear a shelf, or invest in a cart (some baby carts have a changing mat on top). Store bath toys in a well-ventilated laundry hamper.

If you're planning a bathroom from scratch, built-in storage is a boon. In a decent-sized room, a full-height cupboard will hold everything from spare towels to the baby bath. A vanity cabinet, which combines a sink with a cupboard beneath, is a good place to stash diapers or a stool for stepping up to the sink.

Little ones should look forward to bathtime, so make the room cozy. If you are doing a bathroom from scratch, install underfloor heating and a heated towel rail (position this on the wall, rather than at floor level, so little fingers don't get burnt). Flooring and walls should be waterproof, so toddlers can splash around without fuss. Mosaic, *left* **Provide sturdy hooks or a heated towel rail within grabbing distance of the tub, so little ones can wrap up quickly.**

above and top **If you're on a tight budget, an all-white bathroom is a good choice, and can easily be jazzed up with colorful accessories. Bold paintings, plastic toys, or a non-slip rubber bath mat are all good additions.**

ceramic, or limestone tiles are all good choices, as they can be tiled up the side of the tub or even up the walls. Alternatively, choose lino, rubber, or vinyl tiles, which come in bright colors or funky designs. Sanded and painted floorboards are an inexpensive alternative, but avoid carpet, which will just get soggy, or wood veneer flooring.

If you're choosing bathroom fixtures for a children's bathroom, choose a basic white style, with faucets that little ones find easy to turn—chunky levers and cross-head styles are best. Where space is tight, choose a bathtub rather than a shower, as little ones prefer splashing around in the tub. Many companies do tubs designed for small rooms and

Soothing pastels are a restful choice in a family bathroom.

left **In a traditional bathroom, it's less appropriate to have brightly colored accessories. Instead, go with the flow with pretty towels, such as these flower-sprig ones, or gingham or pastel stripes. A big basket is** **useful for extra towels or spare diapers.**
above **For little ones getting in and out, the lower the bath, the better. A small stool also helps. If you want a fabric shower curtain, then line it with a plastic inner curtain.**

this page **Once toddlers can walk, they will quickly want the independence of reaching up to the sink by themselves. Help them to do this by providing a sturdy one- or two-step stool. There are attractive painted wooden ones available, or you could choose a plastic one, which is light and portable. You should also provide tooth mugs, to hold baby toothpaste and brushes. Choose identical tooth mugs, each in a different color.**

this page **Planned for baby twin girls, this bathroom is small, yet incorporates very useful storage. As well as functional cupboards beneath the twin sinks, there are open shelves for extra towels, washcloths, and baskets for toiletries.**

Keep pills and potions out of reach in a lockable medicine cabinet.

a sitz or corner style is guaranteed to appeal to little ones. If you are choosing a full-size bathtub, pick a double-ended style, so when kids are bathing together, one won't get the faucet end. Choose a sink that small children can use easily: a wall-mounted rectangular sink or a classic pedestal style is best.

As for decoration, keep things simple. If there is just one family bathroom, create a space that is soothing for grown-ups once toddlers are in bed. Plain white fixtures teamed with natural surfaces like stone or wood and knocked-back pastels such as blue-gray or taupey pink will provide a stylish backdrop to bright toys and towels. In children-only bathrooms, be bold with color. A tangerine rubber floor, turquoise ceramic tiles, or a funky shower curtain will make the bathroom a fun and stimulating place to be.

below, left to right
User-friendly bathrooms combine a mixture of storage options. Built-in cupboards, hooks, and wall-mounted shelves are all invaluable.

It can come as a shock to have your beautifully planned kitchen infiltrated by baby gear, from a highchair to feeding bottles. But there is a way to blend the two stylishly. Take time to research good-looking seating, equipment and eating utensils, in colors to match your kitchen, and you'll be a long way towards creating a practical and family-friendly eating area.

EATING AREAS

right **If possible, a family kitchen should be big enough to provide a cooking zone and a separate eating and play area. A vintage or rustic style, with unfitted appliances and painted cupboards, creates a relaxed, cheerful mood and easy-care surfaces for little children.**

below **Not all baby tableware has to be plastic. Antique children's cutlery, teamed with metal or wooden platters, will withstand knocks and is highly practical. However, it's important to check that cutlery doesn't have serrated edges that could cut a little mouth.**

In the early months, your baby will be exclusively breast- or bottle-fed and won't even need a highchair, but your kitchen will still require a little rearranging. If you're bottle-feeding, you will need to accommodate a sterilizer and bottles. For many of us, the kitchen becomes the playroom, so do a safety check right now. Anticipate the crawling stage by dealing with trailing wires and fitting socket covers. Find the safest place for a baby to play, well away from the stove or electrical appliances.

Once weaning starts, it won't be long before you need a highchair, although small babies still in need of support may be better off wedged into a "babysitter" seat or a bouncy chair. Purchasing a highchair can be a thorny issue. Some styles are an eyesore and take up too much floor space. Research a chair that looks good in your kitchen. A simple wood style is your best bet. Some highchairs are designed to "grow up" with baby, and transform into a child's seat or a mini table and chair, so can be a sound investment. Reproduction period styles are good in a country kitchen. Pick a highchair that can be drawn up to the family table, as it's lonely for a baby to eat alone.

Once a toddler can sit at the table, ensure surfaces are wipe-clean and practical. If you have upholstered chairs, have cotton loose covers made to protect them, or move them to the

above left **Unbreakable glassware or colorful chunky plastic tumblers are ideal for small children, as they won't break if dropped.**
above right **A highchair helps bridge the gap before a toddler can sit on a kitchen chair.**

For the most stylish family-friendly kitchen, seek out beautifully designed kids' tableware in funky colors, but without cartoon motifs.

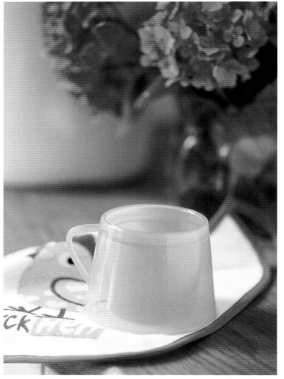

dining room, and buy an inexpensive set of plastic or wood veneer chairs. Safeguard the table top with a wipe-clean oilcloth. In a modern kitchen, a stainless-steel tabletop or a scrubbed pine kitchen table is a practical alternative.

Babies and little children do make a mess when eating, so it can be a good idea to invest in a vinyl "splat mat," which goes directly beneath a highchair to catch any stray food. If you're planning a family kitchen from scratch, choose easy-care flooring that can be cleaned without fuss. A stone floor looks chic, is ultra practical, and can be underfloor-heated. Rubber tiles or lino add a bright splash of color and are comfy underfoot, or opt for sanded and *opposite* **Babies are sociable creatures and don't always want to be banished upstairs to their rooms during the daytime. If there's a quiet nook in the kitchen to keep a second bassinet or a bouncy cradle, let baby nap or play there.**

this page **The secret to a streamlined family kitchen is to plan a home for everything. A breakfast bar is ideal for tucking a highchair or little scooters well out of the way. Later on, older children will enjoy perching up at the bar on tall stools.**

waxed or painted floorboards. Avoid a wood veneer floor, which may scratch easily.

It's amazing how quickly a small child amasses a collection of cups, cutlery, and bowls. Allocate a low cupboard to kids' tableware, then as toddlers become independent they can help themselves. By contrast, once tots are mobile, you'll need to fit safety catches on cupboards or drawers containing potentially dangerous items.

It's fun to choose tableware designed for children. Nowadays there are trendy designs that sit very well in a designer kitchen. If your look is more rustic, enamel bowls, polka-dotted plastic plates, and retro-style pastel cutlery will look good.

A few additions will benefit new families. Invest in a microwave for warming bottles and pureed meals, and don't forget a stereo for nursery-rhyme CDs. Last, but not least, a bulletin board is helpful and makes life feel organized again.

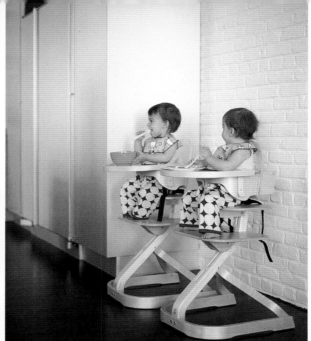

opposite, far left and center **Look out for well-designed baby tableware that combines ease of use for little ones and good looks for you.**

main picture and below **A large table can double up as an eating zone as well as a space for little ones to draw and paint.**

left **Stylish twin highchairs take pride of place in this slick modern kitchen.**

A tiny baby needs little more than a rattle and a soft mat in its waking hours, yet it is never too early to devise a stimulating play area. Toddlers need a place they can call their own, filled with toys and craft materials, and enough space to let off steam, so plan a safe, well-organized zone decorated with imagination and fun.

PLAY ZONES

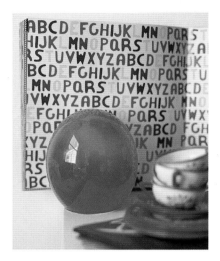

Having enough room at home for a designated playroom is probably every child's (and every parent's) dream. Toys, doll strollers, paints, and more can all be kept together in one place. Yet the reality of family life is rather different. We don't all have a spare room to devote to the children and, besides, modern living means most families prefer to congregate in the kitchen. When children are tiny, you'll also want to keep a close eye on them at all times.

Therefore it makes most sense to plan a play area within a living room or kitchen, or to look for an under-used space that may be transformed into a play zone. These days many of us have an open-plan kitchen/dining room. Is it possible to rearrange the area to create a play corner away from cooking activity? Would you get more use out of a formal dining room or study if it became a family den? If there's a generously proportioned

hall adjacent to the kitchen, or a small sun room off the living room, it may be reinvented as a play zone. Look for spaces that can be fitted with cupboards, so toys are easily tidied away at night, which is especially important if you've taken over a portion of a busy traffic area.

First, mentally divide the area into an active zone and a chill-out corner, and decide how you will allocate the available space. This is important, because if you have busy toddlers they will need a reasonable amount of floor area for pushing toy strollers or building with blocks. Yet a peaceful, safe spot is also important for a baby lying under a baby gym, and little ones in need of some downtime. By thinking through what activities will go on where, you can plan efficient storage, too.

Decoratively speaking, remember that this is an area especially for your children, so do make it fun. You will *left and opposite* **For little ones, most of the action takes place on the floor: balance that decoratively with visual interest on the walls. Here, cupboards are painted with blackboard paint, so children can scrawl away, while art is hung at a higher level.**

right and below **Plan a mixture of storage, from wall hooks to shelves and baskets. Units on castors are useful.**

need to tread a fine line between blending whimsical touches with the existing grown-up décor. For example, a daybed for watching DVDs might be upholstered in a cheerful modern cotton, which acts both as an accent shade in a predominantly neutral interior and looks fun for kids. Likewise, framed colorful abstract art adds a quirky touch to the walls without the need to repaint them in a brighter tone. If sophisticated dark wood or limestone flooring is continuous with the rest of the room, adding a children's-design wool rug will bring softness and character to the new zone.

Adding scaled-down furniture is the most thoughtful way to personalize a play area for tots. It's possible to find lovely mini table and chair sets, from colorful animal-painted designs to vintage styles,

above **If a child has a large bedroom, consider creating a play area in one corner. This can be a particularly good idea for a baby who has much older (and rowdier) siblings, and needs a quiet, cosy place to play. Add a comfortable daybed and a low table that is easy for a toddler to reach.**

left and above **A large open area at the bottom of a staircase makes a spacious play zone. Toys can be tucked under the stairs at night, and a simple mural creates a magical setting.**

A small playroom, linked to an open-plan kitchen via a sliding door, can be closed off for quiet play, or left sociably open.

so pick one that blends in at home. If a tiny table isn't big enough for several toddlers, then buy a junk-store table, cut down its legs, paint it in a zingy color, and accessorize with tiny stools. Low-level soft seating is a brilliant addition for children who spend a lot of time on the floor. Giant beanbags are great for babies, as they provide cozy support, and padded play mats are fun for rolling around on. Also consider seating cubes and floor pillows.

Don't forget to provide somewhere snug for you to sit while reading stories or watching a DVD. If there is room, a two-seater sofa or a daybed is ideal. Add lots of cushions and a soft, washable throw, useful for impromptu daytime naps or just *opposite, left and right* **Once babies make the transition to crawling and then toddling, a playroom must be made safe. This bulletin board is jolly to look at, but is positioned high up, so little fingers can't remove pictures or pins.** *left* **Consider a low seating unit along one wall, fitted with floor-level drawers. Little ones will enjoy sitting on top, if there are plenty of soft pillows.** *above* **Keep an easel out on display, or cover an expanse of wall with blackboard paint, so children can easily indulge in some painting and drawing.**

below **A play zone doesn't have to be huge to satisfy toddlers. This small sun room, off the kitchen and leading onto the garden, provides a safe place for little ones to keep busy. In a traditional-style house, choose an antique cupboard and wicker baskets to conceal toy storage.**

right **If you don't want to compromise on a sophisticated, neutral decorative scheme, remember that toys themselves provide lots of color and charm. In later years, this room will easily transform into a more grown-up den, with shelves for books, and room for a TV and stereo.**

A play area adjacent to the kitchen is both practical and sociable.

right **One end of this little girl's bedroom has been equipped with a tiny table and chairs and mobile book units. It's sensible to keep a sleep zone and play area separate, so a child will settle easily at night.**

snuggling under. In play areas with a TV, ensure that it is positioned low down, so you and the children can watch comfortably, but with the DVD player out of reach of toddlers.

Every play area needs great storage, so that small children can easily access toys and help tidy them away. A floor-to-ceiling shelf unit or a free-standing armoire is a good starting point. Line the shelves with baskets, boxes, or crates, so blocks, Lego, and jigsaws can be quickly sorted. You might want to color-code containers, or stick a picture of each toy type onto the exterior. Small children can't read, but will quickly remember what goes where. Choose

generously proportioned containers, as babies' and toddlers' possessions are often bulky. Keep toys on low shelves, so little ones can help themselves, and store craft materials at a higher level.

Half the fun of a play area is that it is filled with the children's things, so don't be too zealous about tidying things away. Try to allocate enough floor space so that bigger items can be left out ready for the next day's play. It's also a good idea to add a few large baskets or canvas or rubber containers for soft toys. Aim for lightly organized chaos, rather than minimalist splendor, and playtime will be fun for all concerned.

STORAGE

Infants may be small, but they have a multitude of possessions. Long before a new baby arrives, review the available storage space at home and plan for the influx of baby equipment. While you can never have too much storage in a family home, choose wisely. Babies are simple souls and don't need every latest gadget.

right and below **Take time to research the ideal container, from cardboard and plywood to wicker and plastic. A shallow, well-proportioned style makes it easy to find things. Pick an open-topped variety, so you're not continually removing and replacing lids.**

From the moment you pick up your first pregnancy book and read the list of baby's layette, it becomes clear that storage at home will require a radical rethink. Babies are as much part of our fashion-conscious times as adults, and have quantities of trendy tiny clothes to prove it. And that's not all. These days there's a plethora of baby kit, from all the essentials like a stroller and a highchair, to extras such as a playard or portable potty. Toys there will be aplenty. If you are having your first baby, it's also likely that—as your family expands—you'll need to store outgrown clothes or other things for the next sibling.

As you start to amass equipment, perhaps prior to the birth, ask yourself where everything will go. Not everything needs to go in a cupboard: the baby bathtub, baby carriage, bassinet, and car seat, for example, will be in daily use. For these, it's a case of working out where they can live comfortably, without getting in the way. If space is really tight, look for fold-up or more neatly proportioned pieces. In the downstairs rooms, it can be helpful to add a new cupboard, either in the hall or the kitchen, which can hold toy storage boxes, outdoor clothes, modes of transport, and so on.

above left **An office-style chest makes it easy to organize clothes. You can also buy screw-in labels, which are good for labeling drawers and shelves.**
above center **If kids share shelves or an armoire, code containers, with boxes or drawers in different colors.**
above right **A clothes rail needn't be wide, but do allow space at the bottom for increasingly longer clothes.**

below **If there is a deep alcove in the bedroom, design a walk-in closet concealed behind extra-wide doors. A mixture of shelves, drawers, and hanging rails can keep toys and clothes sorted, as well as providing space for extras like a playard or bigger pieces of play equipment. This leaves remaining floor space free for play.**

right **In a modern house, look out for free-standing pieces with a sleek finish, or in a bold color, to blend with other contemporary décor. This glossy wardrobe, in a baby boy's room, will still suit when he is a teenager.**

In the early months, the most pressing issue will be organizing baby's new things. For those who haven't managed to buy a wardrobe before the birth, three giant wicker baskets are an excellent interim measure. Fill one with clothes, one with bedding, and the other with soft toys. If a single chest of drawers is the nursery storage system, choose a style with drawers in a variety of depths. The deep bottom drawer can hold bedding, the middle ones clothes, and the top ones socks, gloves, and hats.

To keep things neat on open shelves, invest in plenty of baskets or boxes (preferably matching). Don't forget that the collection will grow, so buy more then you need now. Opt for a lot of smaller containers, rather than a few big ones, as this makes life easier when it comes to sorting things. Have fun selecting the baskets: there is a huge choice, from woven plastic to wood, acrylic to canvas. Wicker baskets lined with calico or gingham won't snag little garments. If you want to be really organized, label containers according to each category.

It is an investment to choose custom-built storage, but you will find it well worth the expense. In a family home, every inch counts, so tuck a toy cupboard beneath the stairs, add bookshelves around a doorway, or build wardrobes in a

top, left and right **For little ones, cupboards should be accessible at a low level, with grown-up items safe on an upper level.**
above **If possible, conceal the TV in a cupboard—out of sight and out of mind until DVD time.**

A good bookshelf is an essential part of the nursery. Deep, tall shelves are ideal for holding giant picture books.

this page It's hard to imagine the importance of a bookcase when pregnant, but babies need plenty of books from an early age. There are bookcases to suit every wallet: check out home improvement stores for inexpensive wall-mounted varieties, or visit designer stores for trendy free-standing units on wheels. Ensure the shelves are deep, as picture books tend to be big and tall. Baby board books are better gathered into a basket on the floor.

right Display shelves are the best place for photos, special toys, or christening presents.

Choose open-topped or light, easy-to-access containers, so children can help themselves. Pick funky designs that look good and that they will enjoy using.

left and far right, inset **Amass a wide variety of different-size containers, for every room in the house. Look for user-friendly features, such as plastic crates that stack, boxes with handles, and** lidded shoeboxes. Check out chain stores and home improvement stores, which have a good selection of trendy, cheap containers. *below* **Little ones will play with what they can** see, so ensure that there are bowls or baskets filled with favorite things on the floor within grabbing distance. Don't overfill; otherwise things will get in a muddle.

bedroom alcove. The beauty of tailor-made storage is that if you need to store bulky items, such as a playard or a double stroller, you can build a cupboard in just the right proportions so the item fits perfectly.

If you're adding a built-in storage system in a child's bedroom, plan for the long term. Fix shelves on an adjustable system, so they can cater for big picture books now and paperbacks later, and ensure that at least one clothing rail is at a higher level, for older children. It can be a good idea to fill one wall with a combination of wardrobe, bookshelves, and a deep shelf at waist height. In the first few years, the latter creates a useful surface for a changing mat, and later on it will double up as a space for drawing, then a desk for homework. Built-in furniture isn't the sole preserve of modern houses. In a period home, paneled or tongue and groove doors look perfectly in keeping.

Plenty of attractive free-standing pieces of furniture can double up to hold children's things, so it's not necessary to compromise on style.

left and above **Look out for dual-purpose buys, which act as a piece of furniture and hold toys. Plastic stools, lidded chests, and play tables are excellent choices.**

In a retro household, a trendy sideboard is great for holding a TV and DVD player or, for a simple rustic mood, choose an antique toy trunk or a country armoire. Modern furniture in glossy colorful lacquer or steel finishes looks streamlined. Many pieces come in modular units, so you can build up a collection over time. Look out for styles on castors that allow maximum flexibility for altering the layout of a room as children's needs change.

It's also worth scanning children's furniture and mail-order catalogs, for clever, child-size storage options. Some pieces are decorative and fun for the bedroom, such as shelves shaped like a skateboard or castle, a combined child's bench/toy box, or a doll's-house-style open-shelf unit. Other useful storage options will help to organize busy areas such as the hall. A tiered unit, with lots of mini-drawers, a low coatstand, wall hooks, and a combined bench/shoe-rack unit are all excellent ideas for storing endless gloves, coats, and hats.

You will also need to store out-of-season garments, outgrown clothes for younger siblings, or sale buys baby has yet to grow into. If you can, keep these in the attic or spare room. Department stores, specialty storage stores, and mail-order catalogs are a great source of clever storage solutions, from stackable crates to under-bed storage bags.

It's important to be organized, but don't overdo the tidying. A family home, after all, derives much of its personality from the color and character of toys, first paintings, and little clothes hanging from hooks. So combine order behind closed doors, with attractive displays of favorite possessions. Celebrate your children's things and relax. A family home evolves and changes every single day, so accept that and enjoy!

opposite **Children's favorite things add great charm to a room, so show them off on a mantelpiece or shelf.** *left and right* **There's an art to using wall hooks for display. Don't over-crowd, and stick to one type of item, such as clothes and accessories.** *below* **Precious items, from baby shoes to soft toys, should be framed in glass-fronted cases to keep off dust.**

Use the prettiest clothes and accessories to make a decorative display.

CHECKLISTS

Room planning

- Is the potential bedroom big enough to accommodate the basics of a crib, changing table, and feeding chair?

- Do alcoves or spare wall space allow for built-in shelves, a closet, or a custom-made changing table?

- Does the bedroom overlook a noisy street and, if so, can you add double glazing?

- Is the room close to the master bedroom, for easy access at night?

Furniture basics

- Bassinet or cradle.

- Crib or convertible crib.

- Chest of drawers with changing mat, or changing unit.

- Armchair for feeding.

- Beanbags, soft seating cubes, or floor pillows.

- Wall-mounted shelves or a built-in bookcase.

- Wall hooks and hangers, or wardrobe with hanging rail.

Essentials to store in the bedroom

- The changing mat, wipes, diapers, creams, cotton balls and burp cloths.

- Clothing, including bodysuits, one-piece suits, tops and trousers, sweaters, hats, coats, socks, and bootees.

- Changing bag for outings.

- Baby rattles, soft toys, baby board books.

- Bedding, including fitted crib sheets, top sheets, cellular or fleece blankets, a cotton quilt, or baby sleeping bags.

- Gifts and christening presents, including baby clothes waiting to be grown into.

Equipment to store elsewhere

- Infant carrier car seat.

- Baby carriage, stroller, or jogging stroller.

- Baby sling and/or baby backpack carrier.

- Playard.

- Highchair and/or travel booster seat.

- Bouncing cradle and/or baby exerciser.

- Baby bathtub, toiletries, and bath support.

- Bottles, bottle sterilizer, feeding bowls, spoons and bibs.

Essential toy storage

- Rubber tubs, wicker baskets, or canvas containers for loose toys.

- Wall hooks for hanging fabric bags or over-door organizers for soft toys.

- Shelves for books and baskets.

- Space for fabric playhouse or tent, and sit-on cars, doll strollers, and tricycles.

- Toy boxes or crates on wheels for large cars, trains, or building blocks.

- Ottoman or toy chest for baby play nest and/or baby gym.

Safety issues to consider

- Fit plastic socket covers to all electricity sockets.

- Add kitchen cabinet locks and window locks.

- Fit stairgates at the top and/or bottom of stairs.

- Wall-mount a lockable medicine cabinet in the bathroom.

- Tuck trailing wires and blind cords well out of the way.

- Buy a fireguard, but never leave a child near an open fire.

QUESTIONS & ANSWERS

Q: How can I make my baby's room safe?

A: Invest in a new crib, rather than an antique one, and check that it adheres to the correct safety guides. It is also recommended that every new baby have a new mattress. This should fit snugly into the crib or bassinet, with a maximum gap of 1½ inches. It is never too early to fit plastic covers on every electricity socket, so that you're not caught out if baby starts crawling early. If your little one's crib is close to the window, ensure blind cords are short and held well out of the way. For extra safety, fit window catches.

Q: Any good ideas for instant storage?

A: Make the most of hanging options, which are decorative and comparatively inexpensive. Fabric pocket tidies, which can be hung on the back of the door or from hooks, are good for storing tiny items such as socks and bootees, or baby grooming items. Large laundry bags are great for hiding away spare diapers or bodysuits. A fabric crib tidy, which ties directly on to the crib side, is useful for stashing away extra soft toys and keeping spare pacifiers to hand.

Q: Should I introduce ambient lighting?

A: It is always a good idea to add a dimmer switch to the overhead light, so you can settle baby easily. But it's also fun to introduce a secondary light source, as an amusement for your baby, or to provide extra illumination on dark days or for night-time visits. A conventional lamp, with a pretty lampshade, creates a gentle pool of light, but must be located well out of grabbing distance of the crib. For a funkier look, consider a string of tree lights, an LED wall panel, or a revolving magic lantern to cast gentle patterns on the wall. A plug-in nightlight with a pretty motif also provides a comforting glow.

Q: Are there any stylish alternatives to curtains with blackout lining?

A: If you're after a clean, simple look, then shades or shutters are good-looking and highly practical. In a period property with sash windows, consider commissioning a carpenter to build new wooden shutters, which are excellent for keeping out daylight. Plantation-style shutters with adjustable slats, or Venetian blinds, will let in as much, or as little, light as you wish—good for waking up a baby gently. Mail-order or internet blind specialists offer a wide variety of roll-up shades and Roman blinds in everything from denim to flower-emblazoned styles.

Q: Do I really have to have a character-emblazoned plastic changing mat?

A: There are stylish alternatives! If you have a simple, modern scheme, then look for a foam-filled mat in white, or a plain pastel color. Increasingly, it's possible to buy comfortable wedge-shape changing mats that come with a removable fabric cover, in chic variations from piqué cotton to pretty gingham edging, or plain white towelling.

Q: What can I add to stimulate baby?

A: Even tiny babies will appreciate movement and sound to stimulate them while they lie in their crib. Attractive options to try include stringing gingham pennants across the ceiling, or hanging a paper mobile where it will twirl in the breeze, or individual colorful glass chandelier droplets, securely hung to catch the light. A windchime can also be a charming addition. Make sure there are enough soft toys in the crib for baby to play with (ensure they are suitable for babies), and add a wind-up musical mobile. Later on, a crib activity center is fun. It may not be a thing of beauty, but your baby will love it.

NURSERY FURNITURE AND EQUIPMENT

Belly
3003 East Third Avenue
Denver, CO 80206
303 320 1150
www.bellymaternity.us
Furniture and baby bedding from Shabby Chic, the Netto Collection and many more. Also maternity clothes, childrenswear and accessories.

buybuyBABY
1683 Rockville Pike
Rockville, MD 20852
301 984 1122
www.buybuybaby.com
Cribs, cradles, and bassinets, as well as safety equipment.

Casa Kids
106 Ferris Street
Brooklyn, NY 11231
718 694 0272
www.casakids.com
Imaginative designs by architect Roberto Gil. Ingenious chairs, storage and a raised bed, in funky colors.

Ethan Allen Kids
Call 1 888 EAHELP1 or visit www.ethanallen.com for the location of your nearest store.
Cribs and changing tables, as well as decorative accessories such as cute rugs.

For Mercy's Sake
3911 Kandy Drive
Austin, TX 78749
512 665 0882
www.formercysake.com
Handpainted furniture (including cribs), playhouses and storage.

Genius Jones
1661 Michigan Avenue (at Lincoln Road)
Miami Beach, FL 33139
305 534 7622
www.geniusjones.com
Stylish nursery furniture and the best of 20th-century design for children, along with baby accessories, kids' furniture, traditional wooden toys and books.

Giggle
2110 Chestnut Street, between Steiner and Pierce
San Francisco, CA 94123
800 495 8577
www.egiggle.com
Chic nursery goods, from cute cuddly toys to practical items and stylish nursery furniture, including the Stokke Sleepi Crib and pieces from the Netto collection.

Gloria's KidsBeds
1800 Post Road East
Westport, CT 06430
888 600 5437
Space-saving children's furniture, from bunk beds to toy boxes to shelving systems.

The Land of Nod
900 W. North Avenue
Chicago, IL 60622
312 475 9903
Call 800 933 9904 or visit www.landofnod.com for a catalog.
Tasteful cribs, other nursery furniture and dozens more adorable items for babies' rooms, including mobiles, toys, and wall pegs.

Little Colorado
4450 Lipan Street
Denver, CO 80211
303 964 3212
www.littlecolorado.com
Quality handcrafted children's furniture and gorgeous toys, including a kid's kitchen center.

MB Furniture
2311 Avenue U
Brooklyn, NY 11229
718 332 1500
www.mbfurniture.com
Shop online for cribs, bassinets, and highchairs.

Pottery Barn Kids
Call 800 993 4923 or visit www.potterybarnkids.com for the location of your nearest store.
This nationwide chain offers a wide selection of cribs and bassinets, plus bedding that ranges from the pretty to the funky. Also changing tables and nursery seating, rugs, window treatments, storage and accessories.

Wildzoo Furniture
63025 O.B. Riley Road #9
Bend, OR 97701
888 543 8588
www.wildzoo.com
Fanciful children's furniture with practical storage, including junior wardrobes, underbed storage, hooks, and shelves.

YOYAMART
15 Gansevoort Street
New York, NY 10014
212.228.5037
www.yoyashop.com
Ingenious, stylish children's tables and seating, as well as the Netto Collection nursery furnishings. Also groovy crib bedding and cute accessories, including chalkboard paint.

Zac and Zoe
www.zacandzoe.com
Groovy online retailer with elegant cribs, including the stylish Oeuf crib and the versatile Dylan set by Ducduc. Also bedlinen, well-designed wooden toys, play furniture, decorative wall hangings, pillows, mirrors, and play tents.

BEDDING

Amy Coe
www.amycoe.com
Sophisticated, vintage-inspired nursery bedding for little girls and boys.

Babies "R" Us
Call 800 BABY RUS or visit www.babiesrus.com for the location of your nearest store.
Complete line of linens for babies, including the Wendy Bellissimo nursery collection.

Garnet Hill
Call 800 870 3513 or visit www.garnethill.com for a catalog.
Colorful, high-quality crib bedlinen and quilts and baby and toddler clothing in the finest natural fibers. Visit the website for details of their outlet stores.

Kids' Supply Co
1343 Madison Avenue
New York, NY 10128
212 426 1200
www.kidssupplyco.com
Lovely linens and accessories, as well as nursery furniture and cute cribs.

Night and Day
7033 E 1st Avenue
Scottsdale, AZ 85251
480 481 5106
Babies' and children's linens, decorative pillows, and robes.

Rachel Ashwell Shabby Chic
2185 Fillmore St.
San Francisco, CA. 94115
415 771 3881
www.shabbychic.com
Receiving blankets, burp cloths, crib linen and bumpers, and comforters, all in the signature Shabby Chic prints. Also gorgeous accessories such as diaper stackers, bibs, and lampshades.

Westpoint Stevens
Call 800 533 8229 or visit www.westpointstevens.com for a retailer near you.
Bedding for kids and teens, including Disney character bed linen and baby crib sets.

STORAGE

Frick and Frack's Toy Storage
1470 Route 23 North
Wayne, NJ 07470
973 696 6701
www.frickandfrack.com
Handpainted toy benches, rocking chairs, and trunks.

Hold Everything
Call 800 840 3596 or visit www.holdeverything.com for the location of your nearest store.
Everything for storage.

IKEA
Call 800 254 IKEA or visit www.ikea.com for the location of your nearest store.
Kids' furniture and accessories.

Inside Out Productions
10836 Washington Boulevard
Culver City, CA 90232
310 838 0255
www.insideoutproductions.com
Specializes in children's storage chairs.

SOURCES

Wal-mart
Call 1 800 WALMART or visit
www.walmart.com for the location of
your nearest store.
*Wide range of storage, including canvas
totes and woven storage chests in pretty
colors and all shapes and sizes. Also
cute braided rag rugs for kids' rooms,
kids' chairs, bed canopies and more.*

PAINTS

Crayola Paints
Call 800 344 0400 or visit
www.benjaminmoore.com for a retailer
near you.
*Washable latex paint, including glitter,
glow in the dark, and chalkboard
varieties.*

**The Old Fashioned Milk Paint
Co., Inc.**
436 Main Street
P.O. Box 222
Groton, MA 01450
978 448 6336
www.milkpaint.com
*Non-fade colors made to a traditional
milk paint recipe.*

WallNutz
Call 877 360 3325 or visit
www.wallnutz.com for details of your
nearest retailer.
*Attractive, inexpensive, paint-by-number
wall mural kits for decorating kids'
rooms.*

BATHROOMS

Bed, Bath & Beyond
620 6th Avenue
New York, NY 10011
Call 800 GO BEYOND or visit
www.bedbathandbeyond.com for
the location of your nearest store.
Modern bathroom accessories.

The Bumblebee Bush
Call 270 393 BEES or visit
www.bumblebeebush.com
Bath and linens for babies.

Smart-Babies.com
Call 877 310 6647 or visit
www.smart-babies.com
Bath toys.

ACCESSORIES AND GIFTS

Babystyle.com
Call 877 378 9537 or visit
www.babystyle.com for a catalog.
*Nursery furniture, bedding and
accessories.*

ChildSecure
10660 Pine Haven
N. Bethesda, MD 20852
800 450 6530
Safety guidance and childproofing.

Cath Kidston
Brentwood Country Mart
225 26th Street, #33
Los Angeles, CA 90402
310 451 6727
www.cathkidston.com
*Beanbags, towels, bathrobes, wallpaper
and storage boxes and bags in cheerful
florals, dots and retro prints.*

City Cricket
215 W 10th St
New York, NY 10014
212 242 2258
www.citycricket.com
*Blankets, vintage-style toys, and
flatware for babies and kids.*

Cocoa Crayon
Call 212 439 9346 or visit
www.cocoacrayon.com
*Funky bibs, blankets, and burp cloths,
gorgeous blankets and other knitted
goods, and super-chic crib bedding.
Also adorable melamine tableware.*

Kid Carpet
Call 888 308 4884 or visit
www.kidcarpet.com
*High-quality rugs for playrooms
and kids' rooms.*

Kidmodern
Call 718 855 9657 or visit
www.kidmodern.com
*Imaginative, colorful artworks for kids
by artist Gale Kaseguma.*

Oopsy Daisy Fine Art for Kids
Call 619 640 6649 or visit
www.oopsydaisy.com for details of a
retailer near you.
*Quirky, gorgeous artworks especially for
kids by artists including Gale Kaseguma.
Stretched canvases, framed pictures,
growth charts, murals, nightlights, door
decor, and placemats.*

Target
Call 800 800 8800 or visit
www.target.com for the location of
your nearest store.
*This one-stop bargain shopper's
store offers colorful, fun storage
and accessories kids will love.*

Urban Outfitters
Broadway & Bleeker
628 Broadway
New York, NY 10012
Call 212 475 0009 or visit
www.urbanoutfitters.com for the location
of your nearest store.
*Trendy and affordable home accessories,
including decorative wall art, retro storage
boxes, baskets, and wall and over-door
storage hooks.*

WINDOW TREATMENTS

Blinds.com
Call 800 505 1905 or visit
www.blinds.com
*Blinds from major name brands,
including blackout window shades
for nurseries.*

Home Depot
Call 1 800 553 3199 or visit
www.homedepot.com for the location
of your nearest store.
*Window treatments, including colorful
roll-up shades, simple panel drapes,
valances, and plantation shutters.*

Shutter Classic
Call 719 266 1046 or visit
www.shutterclassic.com
*Plantation shutters in painted or
stained finishes.*

All photography by Winfried Heinze

Key: a=above, b=below, r=right, l=left, c=center

1 Josephine Ryan's house in London; **5al** Sophie Eadie's home in London; **5ar** A family home in New York designed by Susan Johnson of Blue Bench; **5b** Josephine Ryan's house in London; **12–13** The Collette's home in Holland designed by architect Pascal Grosfeld; **14** A family home in South London; **15** Elle & Aarrons' rooms on Riverbank, Hampton Court; **16l** A family home in South London; **17** Sam de Teran's family home in West London; **18l & 19l** A family home in South London; **18r** The Collette's home in Holland, designed by architect Pascal Grosfeld; **20–21** A family home in Holland designed by Jaspar Jansen of i29 design; **22–23** Emma Cassi's home in London; **26–27** The home of Graham Turner & Ingrid Koudstaal in Leiden, the Netherlands; **28–29** A family home in Holland designed by Jaspar Jansen of i29 design; **30–31** A Chelsea apartment designed by Studio Azzurro Architects; **34–35** Sophie Eadie's home in London; **36–37** Josephine Ryan's house in London; **38–39** Apple Lydon's bedroom; **40–41** A family home in Manhattan; **42–43** Emma O'Neill's and Ben Cherner's house in Manhattan; **44–45** A family home in Southampton; **46–47** Architect Haifa Hammami's house in London; **48–49** Sophie Eadie's home in London; **50–51** Gabriel's room in South London; **52–53** The Collette's home in Holland designed by architect Pascal Grosfeld; **54–55** Elle & Aarrons' rooms on Riverbank, Hampton Court; **56–57** Gabriel's room in South London; **58–59** A family home in South London; **60–61** Josephine Ryan's house in London; **63** Sophie Eadie's home in London; **64–65** Ella Macpherson of homity's home in Brighton; **66–67** Sam de Teran's family home in West London; **68–69** Ella Macpherson of homity's home in Brighton; **70–71** A family home in North London designed by Wells Mackereth Architects; **72–73** A family house designed by Henri Fitzwilliam–Lay; **74–75** The Sullivan's home in New York; **76–77** The Watts' home in Amsterdam; **78–79** Sam de Teran's family home in West London; **80r** A family home in North London designed by Wells Mackereth Architects; **81b, 82r & 83l** A family house designed by Henri Fitzwilliam–Lay; **83ar** A family home in North London designed by Wells Mackereth Architects; **83br** Elle & Aarrons' rooms on Riverbank, Hampton Court; **84l & 85** Ella Macpherson of homity's home in Brighton; **84r** The Sullivan's home in New York; **86** A family home in New York designed by Susan Johnson of Blue Bench; **87ar** Ella Macpherson of homity's home in Brighton; **87bl** A family house designed by Henri Fitzwilliam–Lay; **87br** Architect Haifa Hammami's house in London; **88–89** The Collette's home in Holland designed by architect Pascal Grosfeld; **90** Josephine Ryan's house in London; **91 al & ar** Sophie Eadie's home in London; **92** Sam de Teran's family home in West London; **93** Architect Haifa Hammami's house in London; **94r–95b** A family home in North London designed by Wells Mackereth Architects; **95a** A family home in New York designed by Susan Johnson of Blue Bench; **96–97** Elle & Aarrons' rooms on Riverbank, Hampton Court; **98–99l** A family home in Brighton, **98a** shows the book *A is For Artist (an alphabet),* Tate Publishing 2004, authored by Silence and Ella Doran; **99r** Elle & Aarrons' rooms on Riverbank, Hampton Court; **100l** A family home in Manhattan; **100r–101ar** A family home in New York designed by Susan Johnson of Blue Bench; **101br** Emma O'Neill's and Ben Cherner's house in Manhattan; **102–103l** A family home in North London designed by Wells Mackereth Architects; **103r** Emma O'Neill's and Ben Cherner's house in Manhattan; **104l** Josephine Ryan's house in London; **105r** A bedroom in Manhattan designed by Roberto Gil of Casa Kids; **106–107** Sam de Teran's family home in West London; **110l** The Silverman/ Marcus residence in New York City designed by Kid's Digs Carol Maryan and Beth Rosenberg; **110r** The Collette's home in Holland designed by architect Pascal Grosfeld; **111al** A family home in Holland designed by Jaspar Jansen of i29 design; **111ar** A Chelsea apartment designed by Studio Azzurro Architects; **111br** Elle & Aarrons' rooms on Riverbank, Hampton Court; **112al** A family house designed by Henri Fitzwilliam–Lay; **112ar** A family home in Brighton; **112b** Sophie Eadie's home in London; **113** The Collette's home in Holland designed by architect Pascal Grosfeld; **115ar** Architect Haifa Hammami's house in London; **120l** The Collette's home in Holland designed by architect Pascal Grosfeld; **121r** A Chelsea apartment designed by Studio Azzurro Architects; **123** The Sullivan's home in New York; **127** A bedroom in Manhattan designed by Roberto Gil of Casa Kids; **128** A family home in Brighton, shows the book *A is For Artist (an alphabet),* Tate Publishing 2004, authored by Silence and Ella Doran.

PICTURE CREDITS

Architects and designers whose work is featured in this book:

Blue Bench
159 Duane Street
New York, NY 10013
USA
t. 212 267 1500
www.bluebenchnyc.com
pages 5ar, 86, 95a, 100r–101ar

Casa Kids
Roberto Gil
106 Ferris Street
Brooklyn, NY 11231
USA
t. 718 694 0272
www.casakids.com
pages 105r, 127

Cherner Design
Architecture & furniture design
(including 'Cherner chair')
Ben Cherner, Principal
t. 212 375 8464
bc@chernerdesign.com
www.chernerchair.com
pages 44–45, 101br, 103r

Emma Cassi
Lace jewellery designer
t.+44 20 8487 2836
www.emmacassi.com
pages 22–23

Grosfeld Architecten
Pascal Grosfeld
Minervum 7489
4817 ZP Breda
The Netherlands
t. +31 76 522 18 11
www.grosfeld-architecten.nl
*pages 12–13, 18r–19l, 52–53,
76–77, 88–89, 110r, 113, 120l*

Henri Fitzwilliam-Lay Ltd
m. +44 7968 948 053
hfitz@hotmail.com
*pages 72–73, 81b, 82r, 83l, 87bl,
112al*

homity
t. +44 1273 672 585
www.homity.co.uk
pages 64–65, 68–69, 84l, 85, 109c

i29 design
Industrieweg 29
1115 AD Duivendrecht
The Netherlands
t. +31 20 695 61 20
www.i29.nl
pages 20–21, 28–29, 111al

Josephine Ryan Antiques
63 Abbeville Road
London SW4 9JW
t/f. +44 20 8675 3900
www.josephineryanantiques.co.uk
*pages 1, 5b, 36–37, 60–61, 90,
104l*

Katie Lydon Interiors
New York, USA
t. 212 226 2690
e. kalershankey@aol.com
pages 38–39

Kid's Digs
212 West 79th Street, Apt 1–C
New York, NY 10024
USA
t. 212 787 7800
page 110l

Malin Iovino Design
43 St Saviour's Wharf
Mill Street
London SE1 2BE
t. +44 20 7252 3542
e. iovino@btconnect.com
pages 14, 16l, 18l, 58–59

Pamplemousse Design Inc
New York, USA
t. 212 980 2033
pages 40–41, 42–43, 100l

Silence
Creative research design
consultancy
t. +44 1273 299 231
www.silence.co.uk
pages 98r–99l, 112ar, 128

Studio Azzurro Architects
Chris & Milla Gough-Willetts
Directors
t. +44 20 7373 2429
t. 415 435 5767
www.studioazzurro.co.uk
pages 30–31, 111ar, 121r

Studio Sofield
Emma O'Neill, Vice President
t: 212 473 1300
www.studiosofield.com
pages 44–45, 101br, 103r

**The New England Shutter
Company**
Sophie Eadie
16 Jaggard Way
London SW12 8UB
t. +44 20 8675 1099
www.tnesc.co.uk
pages 5al, 34–35, 48–49, 63, 91, 112b

Wells Mackereth Architects
5e Shepherd Street
London W1J 7HP
t. +44 20 7495 7055
www.wellsmackereth.com
*pages 70–71, 80r, 83ar, 94r–95b,
102–103l*

INDEX

Figures in italics indicate captions.

ACKNOWLEDGMENTS

It has been fun writing a book on babies' rooms, so thank you Alison Starling and David Peters for commissioning me to do one. Thanks also to my agent, Fiona Lindsay of Limelight Management, for her enthusiastic support.

It isn't easy to photograph a real baby's room without disrupting crucial routines. So thank you, Winfried, for patiently taking beautiful photographs, at break-neck speed, and managing to charm every baby into the sweetest of smiles!

Thank you to Annabel Morgan for perfect editorial direction, Pamela Daniels for elegant design, and Tracy Ogino for inspired locations. And thanks to all the parents whose babies' rooms feature in this book.

Thanks to my parents, Harry and Ann. And, last but not least, thank you to my own family, Anthony, Cicely, and Felix, for all your cheery encouragement, and for always giving me the best welcome home.

The publishers would like to thank all those who kindly allowed us to photograph their families and their homes for this book.